Practical Computer Vision with SimpleCV

Kurt Demaagd, Anthony Oliver, Nathan Oostendorp, and
Katherine Scott

O'REILLY®

Beijing · Cambridge · Farnham · Köln · Sebastopol · Tokyo

Practical Computer Vision with SimpleCV

by Kurt Demaagd, Anthony Oliver, Nathan Oostendorp, and Katherine Scott

Published by O'Reilly Media, Inc., 1005 Gravenstein Highway North, Sebastopol, CA 95472.

O'Reilly books may be purchased for educational, business, or sales promotional use. Online editions are also available for most titles (*http://my.safaribooksonline.com*). For more information, contact our corporate/institutional sales department: 800-998-9938 or *corporate@oreilly.com*.

Editor: Brian Jepson

Production Editor: Iris Febres

Proofreader: Gillian McGarvey

Cover Designer: Karen Montgomery

Interior Designer: David Futato

Illustrators: Robert Romano and Rebecca Demarest

Revision History for the First Edition:

2012-07-23   First release

See *http://oreilly.com/catalog/errata.csp?isbn=9781449320362* for release details.

ISBN: 978-1-449-32036-2

[LSI]

1343141873

Table of Contents

Preface

SimpleCV is a framework for use with Python. Python is a relatively easy language to learn. For individuals who have no programming experience, Python is a popular language for introductory computer and web programming classes. There are a wealth of books on programming in Python and even more free resources available online. For individuals with prior programming experience but with no background in Python, it is an easy language to pick up.

As the name SimpleCV implies, the framework was designed to be simple. Nonetheless, a few new vocabulary items come up frequently when designing vision systems using SimpleCV. Some of the key background concepts are described below:

Computer Vision
> The analyzing and processing of images. These concepts can be applied to a wide array of applications, such as medical imaging, security, autonomous vehicles, and so on. It often tries to duplicate human vision by using computers and cameras.

Machine Vision
> The application of computer vision concepts, typically in an industrial setting. These applications are used for quality control, process control, or robotics. These are also generally considered the "solved" problems. However, there is no simple dividing line between machine vision and computer vision. For example, some advanced machine vision applications, such as 3D scanning on a production line, may still be referred to as computer vision.

Tuple
> A list with a pair of numbers. In Python, it is written enclosed in parentheses. It is often used when describing (x, y) coordinates, the width and height of an object, or other cases where there is a logical pairing of numbers. It has a slightly more technical definition in mathematics, but this definition covers its use in this book.

NumPy Array or Matrix
> NumPy is a popular Python library used in many scientific computing applications, known for its fast and efficient algorithms. Since an image can also be thought of as an array of pixels, many bits of processing use NumPy's array data type. When an array has two or more dimensions, it is sometimes called a Matrix. Although intimate knowledge of NumPy is not needed to understand this book, it is useful from time to time.

Blob
> Blobs are contiguous regions of similar pixels. For example, in a picture detecting a black cat, the cat will be a *blob* of contiguous black pixels. They are so important in computer vision that they warrant their own chapter. They also pop up from time to time throughout the entire book. Although covered in detail later, it is good to at least know the basic concept now.

JPEG, PNG, GIF, or other image formats
> Images are stored in different ways, and SimpleCV can work with most major image formats. This book primarily uses PNG's, which are technically similar to GIF's. Both formats can potentially use non-lossy compression, which essentially means that the image quality is not changed in the process of compressing it. This creates a smaller image file without reducing the quality of the image. Some examples also use JPEG's. This is a form of lossy compress, which results in even smaller files, but at the cost of some loss of image quality.

PyGame
> PyGame appears from time to time throughout the book. Like NumPy, PyGame is a handy library for Python. It handles a lot of window and screen management work. This will be covered in greater detail in the Drawing chapter. However, it will also pop up throughout the book when discussing drawing on the screen.

Conventions Used in This Book

The following typographical conventions are used in this book:

Italic
> Indicates new terms, URLs, email addresses, filenames, and file extensions.

`Constant width`
> Used for program listings, as well as within paragraphs to refer to program elements such as variable or function names, databases, data types, environment variables, statements, and keywords.

`Constant width bold`
> Shows commands or other text that should be typed literally by the user.

`Constant width italic`
> Shows text that should be replaced with user-supplied values or by values determined by context.

This icon signifies a tip, suggestion, or general note.

 This icon indicates a warning or caution.

Using Code Examples

This book is here to help you get your job done. In general, you may use the code in this book in your programs and documentation. You do not need to contact us for permission unless you're reproducing a significant portion of the code. For example, writing a program that uses several chunks of code from this book does not require permission. Selling or distributing a CD-ROM of examples from O'Reilly books does require permission. Answering a question by citing this book and quoting example code does not require permission. Incorporating a significant amount of example code from this book into your product's documentation does require permission.

We appreciate, but do not require, attribution. An attribution usually includes the title, author, publisher, and ISBN. For example: *Practical Computer Vision with SimpleCV* by Kurt Demaagd, Anthony Oliver, Nathan Oostendorp, and Katherine Scott (O'Reilly). Copyright 2012 Ingenuitas, 978-1-449-32036-2."

If you feel your use of code examples falls outside fair use or the permission given above, feel free to contact us at *permissions@oreilly.com*.

Safari® Books Online

 Safari Books Online (*www.safaribooksonline.com*) is an on-demand digital library that delivers expert content in both book and video form from the world's leading authors in technology and business.

Technology professionals, software developers, web designers, and business and creative professionals use Safari Books Online as their primary resource for research, problem solving, learning, and certification training.

Safari Books Online offers a range of product mixes and pricing programs for organizations, government agencies, and individuals. Subscribers have access to thousands of books, training videos, and prepublication manuscripts in one fully searchable database from publishers like O'Reilly Media, Prentice Hall Professional, Addison-Wesley Professional, Microsoft Press, Sams, Que, Peachpit Press, Focal Press, Cisco Press, John Wiley & Sons, Syngress, Morgan Kaufmann, IBM Redbooks, Packt, Adobe Press, FT Press, Apress, Manning, New Riders, McGraw-Hill, Jones & Bartlett, Course Technology, and dozens more. For more information about Safari Books Online, please visit us online.

How to Contact Us

Please address comments and questions concerning this book to the publisher:

O'Reilly Media, Inc.
1005 Gravenstein Highway North
Sebastopol, CA 95472
800-998-9938 (in the United States or Canada)
707-829-0515 (international or local)
707-829-0104 (fax)

We have a web page for this book, where we list errata, examples, and any additional information. You can access this page at:

http://oreil.ly/CompVision_SCV

To comment or ask technical questions about this book, send email to:

bookquestions@oreilly.com

For more information about our books, courses, conferences, and news, see our website at *http://www.oreilly.com.*

Find us on Facebook: *http://facebook.com/oreilly*

Follow us on Twitter: *http://twitter.com/oreillymedia*

Watch us on YouTube: *http://www.youtube.com/oreillymedia*

## CHAPTER 1

Introduction

This chapter provides an introduction to computer vision in general, and the SimpleCV framework in particular. The primary goal is to understand the possibilities and considerations to keep in mind when creating a vision system. As part of the process, this chapter will cover:

- The importance of computer vision
- An introduction to the SimpleCV framework
- Hard problems to solve with computer vision
- Problems that are relatively easy for computer vision
- An introduction to vision systems
- The typical components of a vision system

Why Learn Computer Vision

As cameras are becoming standard PC hardware and a required feature of mobile devices, computer vision is moving from a niche tool to an increasingly common tool for a diverse range of applications. Some of these applications probably spring readily to mind, such as facial recognition programs or gaming interfaces like the Kinect. Computer vision is also being used in things like automotive safety systems, where a car detects when when the driver starts to drift from the lane or is getting drowsy. It is used in point-and-shoot cameras to help detect faces or other central objects to focus on. The tools are used for high tech special effects or basic effects, such as the virtual yellow first-and-ten line in football games or the motion blurs on a hockey puck. It has applications in industrial automation, biometrics, medicine, and even planetary exploration. It's also used in some more surprising fields, such as agriculture, where it is used to inspect and grade fruits and vegetables. It's a diverse field, with more and more interesting applications popping up every day.

At its core, computer vision is built upon the fields of mathematics, physics, biology, engineering, and of course, computer science. There are many fields related to computer vision, such as machine learning, signal processing, robotics, and artificial intelligence. Yet even though it is a field built on advanced concepts, more and more tools are making it accessible to everyone from hobbyists to vision engineers to academic researchers.

It is an exciting time in this field, and there are an endless number of possibilities for applications. One of the things that makes it exciting is that these days, the hardware requirements are inexpensive enough to allow more casual developers to enter the field, opening the door to many new applications and innovations.

What Is the SimpleCV Framework?

SimpleCV, which stands for Simple Computer Vision, is an easy-to-use Python framework that bundles together open source computer vision libraries and algorithms for solving problems. Its goal is to make it easier for programmers to develop computer vision systems, streamlining and simplifying many of the most common tasks. You do not have to have a background in computer vision to use the SimpleCV framework, or a computer science degree from a top-name engineering school. Even if you don't know Python, it is a pretty easy language to learn. Most of the code in this book will be relatively easy to pick up, regardless of your programming background. What you do need is an interest in computer vision, or helping to make computers "see." In case you don't know much about computer vision, we'll give you some background on the subject in this chapter. Then in the next chapter, we'll jump into creating vision systems with the SimpleCV framework.

What Is Computer Vision?

Vision is a classic example of a problem that humans handle well, but with which machines struggle. The human eye takes in a huge amount of visual information, and then the brain processes it all without any conscious thought. *Computer vision* is the science of creating a similar capability in computers and, if possible, to improve upon it. The more technical definition, though, would be that computer vision is the science of having computers acquire, process, and analyze digital images. The term *machine vision* is often used in conjunction with computer vision. Machine vision is frequently defined as the application of computer vision to industrial tasks.

One of the challenges for computers is that humans have a surprising amount of "hardware" for collecting and deciphering visual data. Most people probably haven't spent much time thinking about the challenges involved in sight. For instance, consider what is involved in reading a book. While the eye is capturing the visual input, the brain needs to distinguish between data that represents the book and that which is merely background data to be ignored. One of the ways to do this is through depth perception, which is reinforced by several systems in the body:

- Eye muscles that can determine distance based on how much effort is exerted to bend the eye's lens.
- Stereo vision that detects slightly different pictures of the same scene, as seen by each eye. Similar pictures mean the object is far away, while different pictures mean the object is close.
- The slight motion of the body and head, which creates the parallax effect. This is the effect where the position of an object appears to move when viewed from different positions. Because this difference is greater when the object is nearby and smaller when the object is further away, the parallax effect helps estimate the distance to an object.

After the brain has focused on the book, the next step is to process the marks on the page into something useful. The brain's advanced pattern recognition system has been taught which of the black marks on this page represent letters and how the letters group together to form words. While certain elements of reading are the product of education and training, such as learning the alphabet, the brain's pattern matching is also able to map words written in **several** *different* **fonts** back to that original alphabet (Wingdings notwithstanding).

Take the above challenges of reading, and then multiply them with the constant stream of information through time, with each moment possibly including various changes in the data. Hold the book at a slightly different angle (or tip the e-reader a little bit). Hold it closer or further away. Turn a page. Is it still the same book? These are all challenges that are unconsciously solved by the brain. In fact, one of the first tests given to babies is whether their eyes can track objects. A newborn baby already has a basic ability to track an object, but computers struggle with the same task.

That said, there are quite a few things that computers can do better than humans:

- Computers can look at the same thing for hours and hours. They don't get tired or bored.
- Computers can quantify image data in a way that humans cannot. For example, computers can measure dimensions of objects very precisely and look for angles and distances between features in an image.
- Computers can see places in a picture where the pixels next to each other have very different colors. These places are called "edges," and computers can tell exactly where edges are and quantitatively measure how strong they are.
- Computers can see places where adjacent pixels share a similar color and provide measurements on shapes and sizes. These are often called "connected components"—or more colloquially—"blobs."
- Computers can compare two images and see very precisely the difference between them. Even if something is moving imperceptibly for hours—a computer can use image differences to measure how much it changes.

Part of the practice of computer vision is finding places where the computer's eye can be used in a way that would be difficult or impractical for humans. One of the goals of this book is to show how computers can be used in these cases.

Easy Versus Hard Problems

In many ways, computer vision problems mirror the challenges of using computers in general: computers are good at computation, but weak at reasoning. Computer vision is effective for tasks such as measuring objects, identifying differences between objects, finding high contrast regions, and so on. These tasks all work best under conditions of stable lighting. Computers struggle when working with irregular objects, classifying and reasoning about an object, and tracking objects in motion. All of these problems would also compounded by poor lighting conditions or moving elements.

For example, consider the image shown in Figure 1-1. What is it a picture of? A human can easily identify it as a bolt. For a computer to make that determination, it will require a large database with pictures of bolts, pictures of objects that are not bolts, and computation time to train the algorithm. Even with that information, the computer may regularly fail, especially when dealing with similar objects, such as distinguishing between bolts and screws.

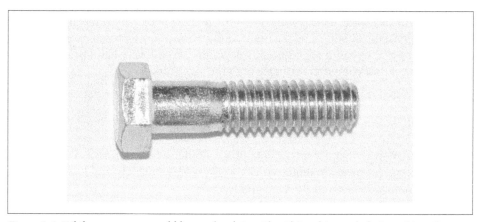

Figure 1-1. While a computer would have a hard time identifying this as a bolt, it could easily count how many threads per inch there are

However, a computer does very well at tasks such as counting the number of threads per inch. Humans can count the threads as well, of course, but it would be a slow and error prone, not to mention headache inducing, process. In contrast, it is relatively easy to write an algorithm that detects each thread. Then it is a simple matter of computing the number of those threads in an inch. This is an excellent example of a problem prone to error when performed by a human, but easily handled by a computer.

Some other classic examples of easy versus hard problems are listed in Table 1-1.

Table 1-1. Easy and hard problems for computer vision

Easy	Hard
How wide is this plate? Is it dirty?	Look at a picture of a random kitchen, and find all the dirty plates.
Did something change between these two images?	Track an object or person moving through a crowded room of other people.
Measure the diameter of a wheel. Check to see if it is bent.	Identify arbitrary parts on pictures of bicycles.
What color is this leaf?	What kind of leaf is this?

Furthermore, all of the challenges of computer vision are amplified in certain environments. One of the biggest challenges is the lighting. Low light often results in a lot of noise in an image, requiring various tricks to try to clean up the image. In addition, some types of objects are difficult to analyze, such as shiny objects that may be reflecting other objects in their surroundings.

Note that hard problems do not mean impossible problems. The later chapters of this book look at some of the more advanced features of computer vision systems. These chapters will discuss techniques such as finding, identifying, and tracking objects.

What Is a Vision System?

A vision system is something that evaluates data from an image source (typically a camera), extracts data about those images, and does something with the results. For example, consider a parking space monitor. This system watches a parking space, and detects parking violations in which unauthorized cars attempt to park in the spot. If the owner's car is in the space or if the space is empty, then there is no violation. If someone else is parked in the space, then there is a problem. Figure 1-2 outlines the overall logic flow for such a system.

Although conceptually simple, the problem presents many complexities. Lighting conditions affect color detection and the ability to distinguish the car from the background. The car may be parked in a slightly different place each time, hindering the detection of the car versus an empty spot. The car might be dirty, making it hard to distinguish between the owner's and the violator's cars. The parking spot could be covered in snow, making it difficult to tell whether the parking spot is empty or not.

To help address the above complexities, a typical vision system has two general steps. The first step is to filter the input to narrow the range of information to be processed. The second step is to extract and process the key features of the image(s).

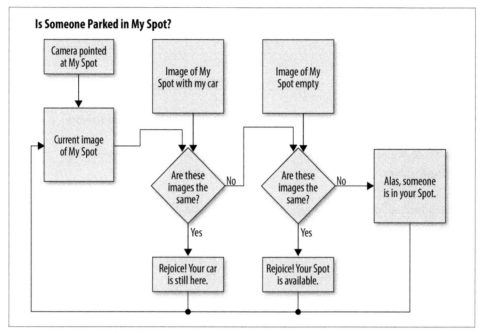

Figure 1-2. Diagram of parking spot vision system

Filtering Input

The first step in the machine vision system is to filter the information available. In the parking space example, the camera's viewing area most likely overlaps with other parking spaces. A car in an adjacent parking space or a car in a space across the street is fine. Yet if they appear in the image, the car detection algorithm could inadvertently pick up these cars, creating a false positive. The obvious approach would be to crop the image to cover only the relevant parking space, though this book will also cover other approaches to filtering.

In addition to the challenge of having too much information, images must also be filtered because they have too little information. Humans work with a rich set of information, potentially detecting a car using multiple sensors of input to collect data and compare it against some sort of predefined car pattern. Machine vision systems have limited input, typically from a 2D camera, and therefore must use inexact and potentially error-prone proxies. This amplifies the potential for error. To minimize errors, only the necessary information should be used. For example, a brown spot in the parking space could represent a car, but it could also represent a paper bag blowing through the parking lot. Filtering out small objects could resolve this, improving the performance of the system.

Filtering plays another important role. As camera quality improves and image sizes grow, machine vision systems become more computationally taxing. If a system needs to operate in real time or near real time, the computing requirements of examining a large image may require unacceptable processing time. However, filtering the information controls the amount of data involved, which decreases how much processing must be done.

Extracting Features and Information

Once the image is filtered by removing some of the noise and narrowing the field to just the region of interest, the next step is to extract the relevant features. It is up to the programmer to translate those features into more applicable information. In the car example, it is not possible to tell the system to look for a car. Instead, the algorithm looks for car-like features, such as a rectangular license plate, or rough parameters on size, shape, and color. Then the program assumes that something matching those features must be a car.

Some commonly used features covered in this book include:

- Color information: looking for changes in color to detect objects.
- Blob extraction: detecting adjacent, similarly colored pixels.
- Edges and corners: examining changes in brightness to identify the borders of objects.
- Pattern recognition and template matching: adding basic intelligence by matching features with the features of known objects.

In certain domains, a vision system can go a step further. For example, if it is known that the image contains a barcode or text, such as a license plate, the image could be passed to the appropriate barcode reader or Optical Character Recognition (OCR) algorithm. A robust solution might be to read the car's license plate number and then compare that number against a database of authorized cars.

## CHAPTER 2

Getting to Know the SimpleCV Framework

The goal of the SimpleCV framework is to make common computer vision tasks easy. This chapter introduces some of the basics, including how to access a variety of different camera devices, how to use those cameras to capture and perform basic image tasks, and how to display the resulting images on the screen. Other major topics include:

- Installing the SimpleCV framework
- Working with the shell
- Accessing standard webcams
- Controlling the display window
- Creating basic applications

Installation

The SimpleCV framework has compiled installers for Windows, Mac, and Ubuntu Linux, but it can also be used on any system on which Python and OpenCV can be built. The installation procedure varies for each operating system. Because SimpleCV is an open source framework, it can also be installed from source. For the most up-to-date details on installation, go to *http://www.simplecv.org/docs/installation.html*. This section provides a brief overview of each installation method.

Regardless of the target operating system, the starting point for all installations is *http://www.simplecv.org/download/*. This page will point you to the latest stable release, and also point you in the right direction for how you can get started with the SimpleCV framework.

Clicking the download button on *http://www.simplecv.org* takes you to a page that automatically downloads the installer for the current computer's operating system. To download the installer for a different operating system, go to *http://sourceforge.net/projects/simplecv/files/* and select the download for the desired operating system. The Windows filename extension is .exe, and the Mac's is .pkg. With Ubuntu Linux, the extension is .deb.

Windows

By far the easiest way to install the SimpleCV framework on Windows is by using the Windows Superpack. Clicking the latest stable release link from *http://www.simplecv .org/download/* will download the Superpack from *http://sourceforge.net*. Simply download the Superpack and follow the instructions. In addition to the basic installation, it will also check for and download any missing dependencies. The following are the required dependencies:

- Python 2.7
- Python Setup Tools
- NumPy
- SciPy
- Easy_install
- OpenCV

The installation creates a `SimpleCV` program group under the Start menu. This includes a link to start the SimpleCV interactive Python shell and a link to access the program documentation. The majority of the examples in this book can be run using the SimpleCV shell. More details regarding the shell are covered in the SimpleCV shell section of this chapter.

Mac

 There have been substantial changes made to the available software and development tools between different versions of Mac OS X. As a result, the installation instructions for Macs are likely to change in response to the ever-evolving underlying configuration of the operating system. Please see the README file included in the software download for the latest installation instructions. You can also view the README file online in the SimpleCV GitHub repository at *https://github.com/ingenuitas/ SimpleCV/blob/master/README.markdown*.

Before beginning a Mac installation, it is strongly recommended that Xcode be installed from Apple. On some versions of Mac OS X, this will resolve dependency and installation errors. To download, see *https://developer.apple.com/xcode*. The SimpleCV framework also requires the Command Line Tools available from within Xcode (Xcode→Preferences→Downloads→Components).

The Mac installation follows a template similar to the Windows approach. From the SimpleCV download page, click the latest stable release link. It will go to Source-Forge.net and begin downloading the installation Superpack. This package will handle the installation of the SimpleCV framework and its major dependencies. The list of dependencies is the same as it is for Windows:

- Python 2.7
- Python Setup Tools
- NumPy
- SciPy
- Easy_install
- OpenCV

Because the SimpleCV framework integrates with Python, the Superpack installs files in places other than the Applications directory. It will also install binary dependencies in /usr/local, and Python libraries in /Library/Python2.7.

The easiest way to work with the examples below is from the Python shell. Once the SimpleCV framework is installed, either click on the `SimpleCV.command` icon in the Applications folder or start iPython from a terminal window. To start a terminal window, go to the Applications folder, find the Utilities folder, and then click on Terminal to launch it. This will bring up a command prompt. At the command prompt, type `python -m SimpleCV.__init__` to bring up the SimpleCV interactive Python shell. Most of the examples in this book can be run from the SimpleCV shell.

Linux

While the following instructions are for Ubuntu Linux, they should also work for other Debian-based Linux distributions. Installing SimpleCV for Ubuntu is done through a **.deb** package. From the SimpleCV download page, click the latest stable release link. This will download the package and handle the installation of all the required dependencies.

Note, however, that even recent distributions of Ubuntu may have an outdated version of OpenCV, one of the major dependencies for SimpleCV. If the installation throws errors with OpenCV, in a Terminal window enter:

```
$ sudo add-apt-repository ppa:gijzelaar/opencv2.3
$ sudo apt-get update
```

Once SimpleCV is installed, start the SimpleCV interactive Python shell by opening a command prompt and entering `python -m SimpleCV.__init__`. A majority of the examples in this book can be completed from the SimpleCV shell.

Installation from Source

Some users may want to have the bleeding edge version of SimpleCV installed. SimpleCV is an open source framework, so the latest versions of the source code are freely available. The SimpleCV source code is available on GitHub. The repository can be cloned from `git@github.com:ingenuitas/SimpleCV.git`.

For a more complete description of using git and the open source site GitHub, see *http://www.github.com/*.

Once the source code is installed, go to the directory where it was downloaded. Then run the following command at the command prompt:

```
$ python setup.py install
```

> Installation from source does not automatically install the required dependencies. As a shortcut for installing dependencies, it may be easier to first install SimpleCV using the appropriate package described above. This does not guarantee that the newest dependencies will be resolved, but it will streamline the process.

Hello World

As is mandated by the muses of technical writing, the first example is a basic Hello World app. This application assumes that the computer has a built-in webcam, a camera attached via USB, or a similar video device attached to it. It will then use that camera to take a picture and display it on the screen.

> The SimpleCV framework uses Python. For those who want a little more background on Python, check out *Learning Python* (O'Reilly, 2007) by Mark Lutz for a good introduction to the language.

```
from SimpleCV import Camera, Display, Image ❶

# Initialize the camera
cam = Camera()

# Initialize the display
display = Display() ❷
```

```
# Snap a picture using the camera
img = cam.getImage()  ❸

# Show the picture on the screen
img.save(display)  ❹
```

Either copy the code above into the SimpleCV shell or save the above code as `hello World.py` using a plain text editor and run the program. For those who have not worked with Python before, these are the basic steps:

1. Open a Terminal window or the command prompt.
2. Go to the directory where `helloWorld.py` is saved.
3. Type `python helloWorld.py` and press the Enter key.

After the program has started, look at the webcam, smile, wave, and say, "Hello World." The program will take a picture and display it on the screen.

This example program uses three of the most common libraries provided by the SimpleCV framework: `Camera`, `Display`, and `Image`. These will be covered in greater detail later in this book; however, a brief introduction to the program follows:

❶ The first line of code imports the libraries used in this program. Technically, `Image` does not need to be specifically listed because Python already knows that `Camera` will return `Image` objects. It is simply included here for clarity.

❷ The next two lines are constructors. The first line initializes a `Camera` object to be able to capture the images, and the second line creates a `Display` object for displaying a window on the screen.

❸ This line uses the `getImage()` function from the `Camera` class, which snaps a picture using the camera.

❹ The final line then "saves" the image to the display, which makes the image appear on the screen.

Hello World purists may object that this program does not actually display the text, "Hello World." Instead, the example relies on the user to say the words while the picture is taken. This situation is easily resolved. `Image` objects have a `drawText()` function that can be used to display text on the image. The following example demonstrates how to create a more traditional Hello World program.

```
from SimpleCV import Camera, Display, Image
import time

# Initialize the camera
cam = Camera()

# Initialize the display
display = Display()

# Snap a picture using the camera
```

```
img = cam.getImage()

# Show some text
img.drawText("Hello World!")

# Show the picture on the screen
img.save(display)

# Wait five seconds so the window doesn't close right away
time.sleep(5)
```

This program appears almost identical to the original Hello World example, except it now draws the text "Hello World" in the middle of the screen. It also has a few new lines: `import time` at the top of the program, and `time.sleep(5)` at the bottom. The `import time` line imports the time module from Python's standard library. The `sleep()` function from the time module is then used at the end of the program to delay closing the window for five seconds.

The SimpleCV Shell

Before going into more depth regarding the features of the SimpleCV framework, this is a good point to pause and discuss one of the best tools to use when working with this book. Most of this book is based on using small snippets of code to do cool things. Yet the traditional way to code is to create a new file, enter the new code, save the file, and then run the file to see if there are errors. If there are errors (and there are always errors), open the file, fix the errors, re-save the file, and re-run the file—and keep doing this loop until all of the errors are fixed. This is an extremely cumbersome process when working with little code snippets. A much faster way to work through the examples is with the SimpleCV shell. The shell is built using IPython, an interactive shell for Python development. This section introduces the basics of working with the shell. Additional tutorials and more advanced tricks are available on IPython's website, *http://ipython.org*.

Most of the example code in this book is written so that it could be executed as a standalone script. However, this code can be still be run in the SimpleCV shell. There are a few examples that should only be run from the shell because they will not run properly as standard scripts. These examples are mainly included to illustrate how the shell works. In these cases, the example code will include the characters >>> at the beginning of each line to indicate that it is expected to be run in the shell. Do not include these initial >>> characters—they are just the shell prompt. For instance, in the shell, the interactive tutorial is started with the `tutorial` command, demonstrated below:

```
>>> tutorial
```

When typing this into the shell, only enter the word **tutorial** and hit the Enter key. Do not type the >>> string. The >>> merely indicates that it is a command to be entered in the shell.

Basics of the Shell

Some readers may have had prior experience working with a shell on a Linux system, MS-DOS, or software like Matlab, SPSS, R, or Quake 3 Arena. Conceptually, the SimpleCV shell has many similarities. Whereas the operating system shells take text-based commands and pass them to the OS for execution, the SimpleCV shell takes Python commands and passes them to the Python interpreter for execution. The SimpleCVshell is based on iPython and automatically loads all of the SimpleCV framework libraries. As a result, it is a great tool for tinkering with the SimpleCV framework, exploring the API, looking up documentation, and generally testing snippets of code before deployment in a full application.

All of the functions available while programming are also available when working with the shell. However, writing code in the shell still has a slightly different "feel" compared with traditional approaches. The shell will interpret commands after they are typed. This is usually on a line-by-line basis, though certain blocks, such as loops, will only be executed after the full block is entered. This places certain practical limitations on the complexity of the code, but in turn, makes an ideal environment for testing code snippets.

Starting the SimpleCV shell varies depending on the operating system. In Windows, there is a SimpleCV link that is installed on the Desktop, or accessible from the SimpleCV folder under the Start menu. From a Mac or Linux machine, open a command prompt and enter `simplecv` to start the shell. After starting the shell, the window should look like Figure 2-1.

If the shell does not start with the SimpleCV command, it is also possible to start it manually. Either enter `python -m SimpleCV.__init__`, or `python` at the command prompt. Then enter the following:

```
>>> from SimpleCV import Shell
>>> Shell.main()
```

To quit the shell, simply type `exit()` and press Return or Enter.

Press the keyboard's up arrow to scroll back through the history of previously entered commands.

Similar to the popular shells found on Linux and Mac systems, the SimpleCV shell supports tab completion. When typing the name of an object or function, press Tab and the shell will attempt to complete the name of the function. For example, if attempting to reference the `getImage()` function of a `Camera` object, first type `getI` and press Tab. The shell will complete the rest of the name of the function. In cases where multiple function names begin with the same letters, the shell will not be able to fully complete the function name. With a `Camera` object, `get` could be referring to `get`

```
+----------------------------------------------------------------+
|  SimpleCV 1.2.0 [interactive shell] - http://simplecv.org      |
+----------------------------------------------------------------+

Commands:
        "exit()" or press "Ctrl+ D" to exit the shell
        "clear" to clear the shell screen
        "tutorial" to begin the SimpleCV interactive tutorial
        "example" gives a list of examples you can run
        "forums" will launch a web browser for the help forums
        "walkthrough" will launch a web browser with a walkthrough

Usage:
        dot complete works to show library
        for example: Image().save("/tmp/test.jpg") will dot complete
        just by touching TAB after typing Image().

Documentation:
        help(Image), ?Image, Image?, or Image()? all do the same
        "docs" will launch webbrowser showing documentation

SimpleCV:1>
```

Figure 2-1. A screenshot of the SimpleCV shell

`Image()` or to `getDepth()`. In such cases, it is necessary to enter additional letters to eliminate the name ambiguity.

 If tab completion does not work, make sure that `pyreadline` is installed.

One of the most convenient features of the shell is the built-in help system. The help system can display the latest documentation for many objects. The documentation is organized by objects, but each object's functions are also documented. For example, the documentation for `Camera` includes general information about the `Camera` class and its methods and inherited methods. To get help using the shell, simply type `help` *object*. For example, to get help on the `Image` object, enter:

```
>>> help Image
```

 Python is case-sensitive: typing `help image` is not the same as `help Image`. This follows a standard convention in programming called CamelCase which is used throughout the SimpleCV framework, and is usually used in Python in general. In many cases, Python modules and class names start with an uppercase first letter, while variables and methods do not.

A slight variation on the above example is using the ? to get help on an object. In the code below, adding a question mark to the end of img will show help information about the image object. Since the SimpleCV shell imports all of the SimpleCV libraries, it is technically possible to skip the line: from SimpleCV import Image.

```
>>> img = Image('logo')
# The next two lines do the same thing
>>> img?
>>> ?img
```

The shell is also a convenient tool for frequently changing and testing blocks of code. In the shell, commands entered are immediately executed. Compare this to the traditional development cycle of writing and saving a block of code, compiling that code—or in the case of Python, waiting for the interpreter to start up—and then actually running the code to examine the results. This traditional process substantially slows any interactive designing and testing. For example, computer vision programming often involves tweaking various filters and thresholds to correctly identify the regions or objects of interest. Rather than going through many write-compile-execute cycles, it is substantially easier to simply test different configurations using the shell.

Consider the challenge of finding blobs. Blobs will be covered in greater depth later, but for the purposes of this example, assume that a blob is simply a region of lighter colored pixels surrounded by darker colored pixels. Letters written in white on a dark background are good examples of blobs. "Lighter" versus "darker" pixels are distinguished based on a threshold value. To ensure that the blobs are correctly identified, this threshold must be tweaked, usually through a process of trial and error.

Image objects have a function named findBlobs() that will search for the blobs. This function has a threshold option that represents its sensitivity. For instance, to find some blobs in the SimpleCV logo, try the following:

```
>>> img = Image('logo')
>>> blobs = img.findBlobs(255)
>>> print blobs
```

The shell will print None because no blobs will be found with the threshold argument set that high. To easily change this, simply tap the up arrow on the keyboard, cycling back through the command history to the line of code that says blobs = img.find Blobs(255). Now replace the 255 with 100, and press the enter key. Then hit the up arrow again until it shows the print blobs line. Hit enter again.

```
>>> blobs = img.findBlobs(100)
>>> print blobs
```

This time, the shell will output something like the following:

```
[SimpleCV.Features.Blob.Blob object at (35, 32) with area 385,
 SimpleCV.Features.Blob.Blob object at (32, 32) with area 1865]
```

This shows that with the lower threshold, the blobs were detected. Later chapters will cover fun blob tricks such as coloring them in and displaying them in a user-friendly fashion. For now, the point is to demonstrate how easy it is to rapidly tinker with the code using the SimpleCV Shell.

The Shell and The Filesystem

One feature of the SimpleCV Shell is that it also includes capabilities of the operating system's shell. As a result, it is possible to navigate around the system without having everything located in the program directory. For example, you can download the images from this book from the SimpleCV website at *http://www.simplecv.org/learn/*. If the images used in this book are then stored in a folder named *SimpleCV* located in the home directory, then the paths to the example images used in this chapter would be: *SimpleCVC:\Users\your_username\SimpleCV\Chapter 2* on Windows *SimpleCV/home/ your_username/SimpleCV/Chapter\ 2* on Linux *SimpleCV /Users/your_username/ SimpleCV/Chapter\ 2* on Mac. There are also other advantages, such as being able to see what types of files are in a directory.

 In the following examples, the Mac/Linux directory and file commands are used. When working in Windows, the forward slash notation is also used, even though the Windows command prompt typically works with backslashes. However, some common Linux commands such as `ls` and `pwd` will still work in the shell on Windows.

The next example shows how to find the image named `ch1-test.png` using the shell, and then load that image. First, locate the correct directory with the following commands:

```
>>> cd
>>> pwd
```

The two commands above should print out the location of the home directory, which is probably */home/your_username* if working on a Linux system, */Users/your_username* on a Mac system, and `C:\\Users\\your_username` on Windows. The example consists of two steps. First, by entering `cd` with nothing after it, the current directory is changed to the home directory. The `cd` command stands for "change directory"; when given a directory path, it moves you to that location. When no path is entered, it moves you to the home directory. The second command, `pwd`, stands for "print working directory." It prints out the current location, which should be the home directory.

Assuming that the SimpleCV folder is located in the home directory, the *camera-example.png* image is loaded with the following command:

```
>>> img = Image('SimpleCV/Chapter 2/camera-example.png')
```

However, when working with a lot of images, it may be more convenient to be in the image directory instead. To go to the directory with the Chapter 2 images, and then output a list of all of the images, type:

```
>>> cd SimpleCV/Chapter 2
>>> ls
```

The result will be a directory listing of all the sample image files. Notice that this works just like using the cd and ls commands in a traditional Linux shell. Not surprisingly, common command options also work, such as ls -la to show the file details as well as all of the hidden files. This is a good way to look up a correct file name and prevent annoying "file not found" error messages. Once the directory and file names are correct, loading and displaying an image is done with the following commands:

```
>>> img = Image('camera-example.png')
>>> img.show()
```

Introduction to the Camera

Having addressed the preliminaries, it is time to dive into the fundamentals of vision system development. For most applications, the first task is to get access to the camera. The SimpleCV framework can handle a variety of video sources and can stream video from multiple devices at the same time. This section will introduce some of the most common ways to access the camera. For greater detail, including how to work with networked cameras and the Kinect, see Chapter 3. Additionally, Appendix B will review several factors to consider when selecting a camera.

The simplest setup is a computer with a built-in webcam or an external video camera. These usually fall into a category called a USB Video Class (UVC) device. This is exactly the case described in the Hello World example in the previous section. In the Hello World example, the following line of code initializes the camera:

```
from SimpleCV import Camera

# Initialize the camera
cam = Camera()
```

This approach will work when dealing with just one camera, using the default camera resolution, without needing any special calibration. Although the Hello World example in the previous section outlined the standard steps for working with cameras, displays, and images, there is a convenient shortcut when the goal is simply to initialize the camera and make sure that it is working, as demonstrated in the following example:

```
from SimpleCV import Camera

# Initialize the camera
cam = Camera()

# Capture and image and display it
cam.getImage().show()
```

This code will behave similarly to the Hello World example, though it is a bit less verbose. An example image is shown in Figure 2-2, but, obviously. actual results will vary. The show() function simply pops up the image from the camera on the screen. It is often necessary to store the image in a variable for additional manipulation instead of simply calling show() after getImage(), but this is a good block of code for a quick test to make sure that the camera is properly initialized and capturing video.

Figure 2-2. Example output of the basic camera example

For many projects, this is all that is needed to access and manage the camera. However, the SimpleCV framework can control the camera in many different ways, such as accessing multiple cameras. After all, if one camera is good, then it follows that two cameras are better. To access more than one camera, pass the camera_id as an argument to the Camera() constructor.

 On Linux, the camera ID corresponds to the */dev/video(number)* device number. On Windows, passing any number to the constructor will cause Windows to pop up a window to select which device to map to that ID number. On Macs, finding the ID number is much more complicated, so it can be easier to simply guess which camera is 0, which is 1, and adjust by trial and error.

```
from SimpleCV import Camera

# First attached camera
cam0 = Camera(0)

# Second attached camera
cam1 = Camera(1)

# Show a picture from the first camera
cam0.getImage().show()

# Show a picture from the second camera
cam1.getImage().show()
```

The above sample code works just like the single-camera version, except now it controls two cameras. The obvious question is: what is the camera ID? The example conveniently uses 0 and 1. In many cases, this will work because 0 and 1 frequently are the camera IDs. If necessary, it is possible to look up these numbers, which are assigned by the operating system. On Linux, all peripheral devices have a file created for them in the /dev directory. For cameras, the file names start with video and end with the camera ID, such as **/dev/video0** and **/dev/video1**. The number at the end equals the camera ID. In Windows, the camera ID number corresponds to the order of the DirectShow devices, which is a bit more complicated to find. So with Windows, passing in any number as the camera ID results in a pop- up window for selecting the appropriate camera device. The ID on a Mac is even harder to find. It is most easily found with trial and error. The ID numbers should start at 0.

Of course, finding the list of camera IDs still does not identify which camera corresponds to which ID number. For a programmatic solution, capture a couple images and label them. For example:

```
from SimpleCV import Camera

# First attached camera
cam0 = Camera(0)

# Second attached camera
cam1 = Camera(1)

# Show a picture from the first camera
img0 = cam0.getImage()
img0.drawText("I am Camera ID 0")
img0.show()

# Show a picture from the first camera
img1 = cam1.getImage()
img1.drawText("I am Camera ID 1")
img1.show()
```

In addition to the basic initialization, the SimpleCV framework can control many other camera properties. An easy example is forcing the resolution. Almost every webcam supports the standard resolutions of 320×240, and 640×480 (often called "VGA" resolution). Many newer webcams can handle higher resolutions such as 800×600, 1024×768, 1200×1024, or 1600×1200. Many webcams list higher resolutions that are "digitally scaled" or "with software enhancement," but these do not contain any more information than the camera's native resolution.

Rather than relying on the default resolution of the camera, sometimes it is helpful to force a resolution to a set of known dimensions. For example, the previous draw Text() function assumes that the text should be drawn at the center of the screen. The text can be moved to different (x, y) coordinates, but an obvious prerequisite for that is knowing the actual image size. One solution is to force the resolution to a known size.

Here is an example of how to move text to the upper left quadrant of an image, starting at the coordinates (160, 120) on a 640×480 image:

```
from SimpleCV import Camera

cam = Camera(0, { "width": 640, "height": 480 })

img = cam.getImage()
img.drawText("Hello World", 160, 120)

img.show()
```

The resulting output will appear like Figure 2-3. Notice the text "Hello World" in the upper-left corner.

The above example is similar to the Hello World program, except that the text is moved. Notice that the camera's constructor passed a new argument in the form of {"key": value}. The Camera() function has a properties argument for basic camera calibration. Multiple properties are passed in as a comma delimited list, with the entire list enclosed in brackets. Note that the camera ID number is NOT passed inside the brackets, since it is a separate argument. The configuration options are:

- width and height
- brightness
- contrast
- saturation
- hue
- gain
- exposure

The available options are part of the computer's UVC system. In addition, the configuration options are dependent on the camera and the drivers. Not all cameras support all of the options listed above.

Figure 2-3. Example of Hello World application with the "Hello World" text

The show() function is used to display the image to the screen. It keeps the image on the screen until the program terminates—or until the shell closes. Clicking the Close button on the window does not close the window. To get more control of the window, use the Display object, which is covered later in this chapter.

The USB Video Device Class (UVC)

UVC has emerged as a "device class" which provides a standard way to control video streaming over USB. Most webcams today are now supported by UVC, and do not require additional drivers for basic operation. Not all UVC devices support all functions, so when in doubt, tinker with the camera in a program like guvcview or Skype to see what works and what does not.

A Live Camera Feed

A good first step when setting up a vision system is to view what the camera is capturing. To get live video feed from the camera, use the live() function. This is as simple as:

```
from SimpleCV import Camera

cam = Camera()
cam.live()
```

In addition to displaying live video feed, the `live()` function has two other very useful properties. The live feed makes it easy to find both the coordinates and the color of a pixel on the screen. This information will be useful in later chapters when cropping images by their coordinates or segmenting images based on color. Being able to click on the live feed to find the coordinates for cropping the image is a lot easier than a trial and error method of guessing what the coordinates or colors are and then tweaking the code based on the results.

To get the coordinates or color for a pixel, use the `live()` function as outlined in the example above. After the window showing the video feed appears, click the left mouse button on the image for the pixel of interest. The coordinates and color for the pixel at that location will then be displayed on the screen and also output to the shell. The coordinates will be in the `(x, y)` format, and the color will be displayed as an RGB triplet `(R,G,B)`. An example is shown in Figure 2-4. The small text on the left of the image is displaying the coordinates and the RGB color values for where the left mouse button was clicked.

Figure 2-4. Demonstration of the live feed

The Display

As much fun as loading and saving images may be, at some point it is also nice to see the images. The SimpleCV framework has two basic approaches to showing images:

- Displaying them directly in a window
- Opening a web browser to display the image

The first approach, showing the image in a window, has been previously demonstrated with the `show()` command. Displaying the image in a web browser is similar:

```
from SimpleCV import Image

img = Image("logo")
```

```
# This will show the logo image in a web browser
img.show(type="browser")
```

Notice that it uses the same show() function, but requires the argument: type="browser". The major difference between the browser and the window is that the window can capture events, such as a signal to close the window. So far, the examples in this chapter have assumed that the window should remain open until the program completes. For larger and more complex programs, however, this might not be the case.

The next example shows how to take more control over when the window is displayed. First, consider the following condensed example, which is similar to the code used earlier in the chapter:

```
from SimpleCV import Display, Image

display = Display()

# Write to the display
Image("logo").save(display)
```

In this case, the user will not be able to close the window by clicking the close button in the corner of the window. The image will continue to be displayed until the program terminates, regardless of how the user interacts with the window. When the program terminates, it will naturally clean up its windows. To control the closing of a window based on the user interaction with the window, use the Display object's isDone() function.

```
from SimpleCV import Display, Image
import time

display = Display()
Image("logo").save(display)
print "I launched a window"

# This while loop will keep looping until the window is closed
while not display.isDone():
    time.sleep(0.1)

print "You closed the window"
```

 Notice how the line "time.sleep(0.1)" is indented after the while statement? That indentation matters. Python groups statements together into a block of code based on the indentation. So it's that indentation that tells Python to execute the "time.sleep(0.1)" statement as the body of the while loop.

The print statement in the example above outputs to the command prompt, and not the image. The drawText function is used for writing text on the image. The print command, on the other hand, is used for outputting text to the command prompt.

Event handling does more than simply close windows. For example, it is relatively easy to write a program that draws a circle wherever the user clicks on the image. This is done by using the mouse position and button state information that is provided by the Display object.

While the window is open, the following information about the mouse is available:

mouseX *and* mouseY
> The coordinates of the mouse

mouseLeft, mouseRight, *and* mouseMiddle
> Events triggered when the left, right, or middle buttons on the mouse are clicked

mouseWheelUp *and* mouseWheelDown
> Events triggered then the scroll wheel on the mouse is moved

The following example shows how to draw on a screen using the information and events listed above.

 To use indented code in the shell, it helps to use the %cpaste macro. From the shell, enter %cpaste, copy and paste the desired code into the shell, and then on a new line enter -- (two minus signs). It will then execute the pasted block of code. This resolves any indentation errors thrown by the shell.

```
from SimpleCV import Display, Image, Color

winsize = (640,480)
display = Display(winsize)   ❶

img = Image(winsize)   ❷
img.save(display)

while not display.isDone():
    if display.mouseLeft:   ❸
        img.dl().circle((display.mouseX, display.mouseY), 4,
                Color.WHITE, filled=True)   ❹
        img.save(display)
        img.save("painting.png")
```

This example uses several new techniques:

❶ This first step is a little different than the previous examples for initializing the window. In this case, the display is given the tuple (640, 480) to specifically set the display size of the window. This creates an empty window with those dimensions.

❷ The same 640×480 tuple is used to create a blank image.

❸ This code checks to see if the application has received a message that the left mouse button has been clicked.

Figure 2-5. Example using the drawing application

❹ If the button is clicked, draw the circle. The image has a drawing layer, which is accessed with the `dl()` function. The drawing layer then provides access to the `circle()` function. The following are the arguments passed to the `circle()` function, in order of appearance: the tuple representing the coordinates for the center of the circle (in this case, the coordinates of the mouse), the desired radius for the circle in pixels (4), the color to draw the circle in (white), and a boolean value for the `fil led` argument which determines whether or not to fill in the circle or leave the center empty.

The little circles from the drawing act like a paint brush, coloring in a small region of the screen wherever the mouse is clicked. In this way, example code acts like a basic painting application that can be used to draw exciting pictures like the one in Figure 2-5.

This example provides a basic overview of working with the display and introduces the drawing layer. For more complex features regarding drawing layers, please see Chapter 7.

Examples

This section provides several straightforward examples of how to capture images, save them to disk, and render them on the display. As we progress, more advanced applications are covered in later chapters. Comments are included in the code to provide guidance about what is happening at each step along the way.

The examples below also use the time module from Python's standard library, which we first introduced in the updated Hello World program. Experienced Python programmers may already be familiar with this module. In these examples, it is used to create timers that cause a program to wait for a specified interval of time. For instance, one example below captures an image every second. The timer is used to control the interval between snapping new photos.

The following examples include the following:

- How to capture images at a fixed interval for time-lapse photography
- How to create a photo booth application that lets users interact with the screen to capture images

 Although most of the code snippets presented in this chapter are designed for convenient use in the shell, these examples are best run as independent Python scripts.

Time-Lapse Photography

This example operates like a camera with a timer: it takes a picture once per minute. It is a simple application that does nothing but save the images to disk. A more advanced version, though, could try to detect if there is any movement or look for changes in the objects. If left running indefinitely, it could quickly consume a great deal of disk space so a limit is included to only snap ten photos.

 Sometimes the shell has problems when code that requires formatting, such as loops, are copied and pasted into the shell. To solve this problem, from the shell enter cpaste, press Enter, then paste the desired code. Finally, type two dashes (--) on a line by itself to exit the paste mode.

```
from SimpleCV import Camera, Image
import time

cam = Camera()

# Set the number of frames to capture
numFrames = 10

# Loop until we reach the limit set in numFrames
for x in range(0, numFrames):
    img = cam.getImage()  ❶

    filepath = "image-" + str(x) + ".jpg"  ❷
    img.save(filepath)  ❸
    print "Saved image to: " + filepath

    time.sleep(60)
```

❶ Snap a picture just like in any other application.

❷ Set up a unique filename so that the image is not overwritten every time. To create unique names, the name is prefixed with image- followed by its sequence through the loop.

❸ Finally, save the image to the disk, based on the unique file name.

A Photo Booth Application

The next example is a simple photo booth application. After all, nothing says, "I'm an aspiring vision system developer" better than getting close with a friend or loved one and taking silly pictures. This application takes a continuous feed of images. When clicking the left mouse button on an image, it saves it to disk as photobooth0.jpg, photobooth1.jpg, and so on.

```
from SimpleCV import Camera, Display, Color
import time

# Initialize the camera
cam = Camera()

# Initialize the display
display = Display()

# Take an initial picture
img = cam.getImage()   ❶

# Write a message on the image
img.drawText("Left click to save a photo.",
        color=Color().getRandom())   ❷

# Show the image on the display
img.save(display)

time.sleep(5)   ❸

counter = 0
while not display.isDone():
    # Update the display with the latest image
    img = cam.getImage()   ❹

    img.save(display)

    if display.mouseLeft:
        # Save image to the current directory
        img.save("photobooth" + str(counter) + ".jpg")   ❺

        img.drawText("Photo saved.", color=Color().getRandom())   ❻

        img.save(display)

        time.sleep(5)

        counter = counter + 1
```

❶ When the application is started, an initial picture is taken.

❷ Instructions are written on the image using the drawText() function. Because no coordinates are passed to drawText(), the message will be written in the center of the screen. The Color().getRandom() function is used to pass a random color to the color argument. This will result in the text being in a different color each time the message is displayed. Then the image is "saved" to the screen. The time.sleep() is used to freeze the image and keep the message on the screen for a few seconds

❸ Wait for a few seconds to allow the user view their image.

❹ Inside the while loop, the image is repeatedly updated. This loop continues until the window is closed.

❺ If the display receives a click from the left mouse button, as indicated by display.mouseLeft, then save the image as photobooth(*number*).jpg.

❻ After the image is saved to disk, a message is written to the screen indicating that the image was saved. It is important to write the text after saving the file. Otherwise, the message would be included on the saved image.

## CHAPTER 3

Image Sources

This chapter examines various video and image sources in more detail. This is an important prerequisite to image processing. Obviously having a source of images is helpful before processing any images. The SimpleCV framework can capture images from a variety of image sources, ranging from a standard webcam to the Microsoft Kinect. In particular, this chapter covers:

- A review of working with webcams
- How to use a Kinect to capture depth information for basic 3D processing
- Using an IP camera as a digital video source
- Working with virtual devices to process images from video feeds or pre-captured sets of images
- How to handle a single image and a set of images

Overview

The SimpleCV framework supports most cameras that connect to a computer through a variety of interfaces such as USB, FireWire, or a built-in webcam. It can access networked IP cameras that are connected via a wire or a wireless connection. It can even interact with many video capture boards, which work with a variety of analog video inputs (such as Composite, Component, and S-Video).

Outside of connecting to the camera, there are options such as whether to use a monochrome or a color camera, or whether to use a camera with a CCD or a CMOS image sensor. Some cameras record different portions of the light spectrum, such as visible, infrared, or ultraviolet. Then there's always the choice of how much to invest, as cameras these days range from the very inexpensive to the very expensive. With all of these options, it is easiest just to start with a basic webcam or even just a local image file. For those who would like more help on how to select a camera that aligns with project requirements, see Appendix B.

This chapter revisits how to work with a locally connected camera, which was first introduced in Chapter 2. It then delves into more advanced topics such as using a Kinect to collect 3D depth information, working with remote cameras on the Internet, and using virtual video devices to do things like accessing streams of data previously saved to disk.

Images, Image Sets, and Video

The SimpleCV framework does not need a camera to process images. Instead, it makes it easy to load and save images that were previously captured and saved to disk. This is useful both for working with pre-existing image sources, and for saving images captured from a camera so they can be processed at a later time. The following demonstrates the three ways to load image files:

```
from SimpleCV import Image

builtInImg = Image("logo")  ❶

webImg = Image("http://simplecv.s3.amazonaws.com/simplecv_lg.png")  ❷

localImg = Image("image.jpg")  ❸
```

❶ Loading one of the built-in images that are distributed with the SimpleCV framework.

❷ Loading an image directly from the Internet by specifying the URL of the image.

❸ Loading an image available on the hard drive by specifying the filename of the image.

The first approach in the above example loads the SimpleCV logo, which is bundled with the SimpleCV software. Additional bundled images include:

simplecv
: The SimpleCV logo

logo
: Also the SimpleCV logo

logo_inverted
: An inverted version of the logo

logo_transparent
: A version of the logo with a transparent background

lenna
: The "Lenna" image found in many common image processing texts

Examples of these are demonstrated in Figure 3-1.

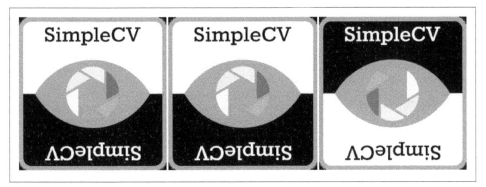

Figure 3-1. Built-in images: simplecv, logo (same as simplecv), and logo_inverted

Saving an image is just as easy as loading one. In general, saving is done by passing the filename to the **save()** function. As a shortcut, if the image was already loaded from the disk, simply calling the **save()** function with no parameters will overwrite the original image. Alternatively, passing a new filename will save a new copy of the image to the disk. To demonstrate some of the options:

```
from SimpleCV import Image

img = Image("chicago.png")  ❶
img.save()  ❷

# Now save as .jpg
img.save("chicago.jpg")  ❸

# Re-saves as .jpg
img.save()  ❹
```

❶ Load the file `chicago.png`.

❷ This saves the file using the original filename, `chicago.png`.

❸ This now saves the image as a new file called `chicago.jpg`. Notice the change in the file extension. It is automatically converted and saved in the JPEG format.

❹ Because the last file touched was `chicago.jpg`, this will save `chicago.jpg`, and not `chicago.png`.

 When saving a file loaded from the built-in images or fetched directly from the Internet, a filename must be provided.

The SimpleCV image library actually looks at the file extension provided to determine the image format. Hence a file with a `.jpg` extension will be saved as a JPEG and a `.png` extension will be saved as a PNG. This is done independently of the file's original format. For example, the following code is an easy way to convert an image from a JPEG to a PNG. The file extension is not case-sensitive for determining the file format, but it does affect the filename. Using `img.save("myfile.PNG")` and `img.save("myfile.png")` will both create a PNG file, but the filenames will preserve the caps.

```
from SimpleCV import Image

img = Image("my_file.jpg")
img.save("my_file.png")
```

Sets of Images

In addition to working with a single image file, it is also a common task to work with a large number of image files. Rather than loading them individually, the `ImageSet()` library manages sets of images. The following example demonstrates how to use an `ImageSet` to manage the saving of a set of files from a security camera. The `ImageSet()` command takes one optional parameter: the path to the directory containing the images to be loaded. If a directory argument is not provided, `ImageSet` will create an empty list to which images can be added.

```
from SimpleCV import Camera, ImageSet
import time

cam = Camera()

camImages = ImageSet()   ❶

# Set to a maximum of 10 images saved
# Feel free to increase, but beware of running out of space
maxImages = 10

for counter in range(maxImages):
    # Capture a new image and add to set
    img = cam.getImage()

    camImages.append(img)   ❷

    # Show the image and wait before capturing another
    img.show()

    time.sleep(6)

camImages.save(verbose=True)   ❸
```

❶ Initialize an empty `ImageSet` object. Images will be added to this object later in the code.

❷ Append the image to the `ImageSet` named *camImages*.

❸ Save the images to disk. Because the images did not previously have a filename, one is randomly assigned. It will be a string of random letters followed by .png. By passing verbose=True to the save() function, it will show the names of the files.

As a final note on ImageSets; like an Image, an ImageSet also has a show() function. Where the show() function displays a single image when called on an Image object, it will show a slideshow when called on an ImageSet object. In the case of ImageSets, the show function takes one argument that sets the number of seconds to pause between images. For example, ImageSet().show(5) will display a slide show with a five=-second delay between showing each image in the set.

The Local Camera Revisited

We first looked at working with a locally connected camera in the "Hello World" program in Chapter 2. For reference, here is that program again:

```
from SimpleCV import Camera, Display, Image

# Initialize the camera
cam = Camera()

# Initialize the display
display = Display()

# Snap a picture using the camera
img = cam.getImage()

# Show the picture on the screen
img.save(display)
```

The salient points to remember here are:

• To work with a locally connected camera, first import the Camera class
• Then use the Camera() constructor to initialize a camera object

The XBox Kinect

Historically, the computer vision market has been dominated by 2D vision systems. 3D cameras were often expensive, relegating them to niche market applications. More recently, however, basic 3D cameras have become available on the consumer market, most notably with the XBox Kinect. The Kinect is built with two different cameras. The first camera acts like a traditional 2D 640×480 webcam. The second camera generates a 640×480 depth map, which maps the distance between the camera and the object. This obviously will not provide a Hollywood style 3D movie, but it does provide an additional degree of information that is useful for things like feature detection, 3D modeling, and so on.

Want to play with Kinect code without owning a Kinect? The Freenect project has a set of drivers called *fakenect* which fake the installation of a Kinect. For more information, see *http://openkinect.org*.

Installation

The Open Kinect project provides provides free drivers that are required to use the Kinect. The standard installation on both Mac and Linux includes the Freenect drivers, so no additional installation should be required. For Windows users, however, additional drivers must be installed. Because the the installation requirements from Open Kinect may change, please see their website for installation requirements at *http://open kinect.org*.

Using the Kinect

As mentioned above, the Kinect is a combination of a standard 2D camera with a second depth sensor to capture 3D information. The overall structure of working with the 2D camera is similar to a local camera. However, initializing the camera is slightly different:

```
from SimpleCV import Kinect

# Initialize the Kinect
kin = Kinect()   ❶

# Snap a picture with the Kinect
img = kin.getImage()   ❷

img.show()
```

❶ Unlike local cameras, which are initialized by calling the `Camera()` constructor, the Kinect is initialized with the `Kinect()` constructor. If the drivers were not correctly installed, this line of code will print a warning and future operations will fail. Note that unlike `Camera()`, the `Kinect()` constructor does not take any arguments.

❷ Although the initialization is different, the basic steps for capturing an image are the same. Simply call `getImage()` from the Kinect object to snap a picture with the Kinect's 2D camera.

Using the Kinect simply as a standard 2D camera is a pretty big waste of money. The Kinect is a great tool for capturing basic depth information about an object. Underneath the hood, it measures depth as a number between 0 and 1023, with 0 being the closest to the camera and 1023 being the farthest away. Although the Kinect captures values in a range from 0 to 1023, the SimpleCV framework automatically scales that range down to a 0 to 255 range. Why? Instead of treating the depth map as an array of numbers, it is often desirable to display it as a grayscale image. In this visualization, nearby objects will appear as dark grays, whereas objects in the distance will be light gray or white. To better understand this, the following example demonstrates how to extract depth information:

```
from SimpleCV import Kinect

# Initialize the Kinect
kin = Kinect()

# This works like getImage, but returns depth information
depth = kin.getDepth()

depth.show()
```

The example output, shown in Figure 3-2, shows some hints of a person in the foreground, as indicated by the darker person-shaped spot. Other, more distant objects are also somewhat discernible further in the background. The image is not a traditional picture, but the relative distance of the objects still provides some indication or outline of the actual objects.

Figure 3-2. A depth image from the Kinect

The Kinect's depth map is scaled so that it can fit into a 0 to 255 grayscale image. This reduces the granularity of the depth map. If needed, however, it is possible to get the original 0 to 1023 range depth map. The function getDepthMatrix() returns a NumPy matrix with the original full range of depth values. This matrix represents the 2×2 grid of each pixels depth. More information about the link between matrices and images is covered in Chapter 4.

```
from SimpleCV import Kinect

# Initialize the Kinect
kin = Kinect()

# This returns the 0 to 1023 range depth map
depthMatrix = kin.getDepthMatrix()

print depthMatrix
```

Kinect Examples

Putting the pieces together, it is possible to create a real-time depth camera video feed using the Kinect. These examples are best run as a separate Python script, rather than in the SimpleCV shell. The three examples are:

- A video feed of the Kinect depth map
- Using the Kinect to identify and extract just the part of an image in the foreground
- Using the Kinect to measure an object that passes into its field of view

The first example is a basic streaming feed from the Kinect. Like the examples in Chapter 2 that used the webcam to create a video feed, this provides a real-time stream of images. Unlike the previous examples, however, it shows the depth map instead of the actual image.

```
from SimpleCV import Kinect

# Initialize the Kinect
kin = Kinect()

# Initialize the display
display = kin.getDepth().show()

# Run in a continuous loop forever
while (True):
    # Snaps a picture, and returns the grayscale depth map
    depth = kin.getDepth()

    # Show the actual image on the screen
    depth.save(display)
```

Networked Cameras

The previous examples in this book have assumed that the camera is directly connected to the computer. However, the SimpleCV framework can also control Internet Protocol (IP) Cameras. Popular for security applications, IP cameras contain a small web server and a camera sensor. They then stream the images from the camera over a web feed.

As of the writing of this book, these cameras have recently dropped substantially in price. Low end cameras can be purchased for as little as $30 for a wired camera and $60 for a wireless camera.

Most IP cameras support a standard HTTP transport mode, and stream video via the Motion JPEG (MJPG) format. To access a MJPG stream, use the `JpegStreamCamera` library. The basic setup is the same as before, except that now the constructor must provide the address of the camera and the name of the MJPG file. This is represented by *mycamera* and *video.mjpg*, respectively, in the example below:

```
from SimpleCV import JpegStreamCamera

# Initialize the webcam by providing URL to the camera
cam = JpegStreamCamera("http://mycamera/video.mjpg")

cam.getImage().show()
```

In general, initializing an IP camera requires the following information:

- The IP address or hostname of the camera, represented by *mycamera* in the example above.
- The path to the Motion JPEG feed, represented by *video.mjpg* in the example above.
- The username and password, if required. This configuration option is demonstrated below.

 Having difficulty accessing an IP camera? Try loading the URL in a web browser. It should show the video stream. If the video stream does not appear, it may be that the URL is incorrect or that there are other configuration issues. One possible issue is that the URL requires a login to access it, which is covered in more detail below.

 Many phones and mobile devices today include a built-in camera. Tablet computers and both the iOS and Android smart phones can be used as network cameras with apps that stream the camera output to an MJPG server. To install one of these apps, search for "IP Camera" in the app marketplace on an iPhone/iPad or search for "IPCAM" on Android devices. Some of these apps are for viewing feeds from other IP cameras, so make sure that the app is designed as a server and not a viewer.

The first configuration parameter needed is the IP or hostname of the network camera, which varies from model to model. The camera manual should list this, though the exact configuration is based on both the camera's default configuration and the local network's configuration. The IP or hostname used is exactly the same as the IP or hostname used when accessing the camera via a web browser.

The next step is to find the name of the video stream file, which should end in `.mjpg`. Once the camera is online, log in to the camera from a web browser. Popular username-password pairs are `admin/admin` or `admin/1234`, although this information should be provided in the camera documentation. After logging in, the web page will most likely display the video stream. If it does not, navigate to the page that does show the video stream. Then right click on the streaming video and copy the URL. If the stream's URL is not available by right-clicking, it may require a little detective work to find the MJPG stream URL for the camera. To see an initial database for some popular cameras, go to: *https://github.com/ingenuitas/SimpleCV/wiki/List-of-IP-Camera-Stream-URLs.*

If the video stream requires a username and password to access it, then provide that authentication information in the URL as shown below. In the example URL, the text string `admin` should be replaced with the actual username; the string `1234` should be replaced with the actual password; the string `192.168.1.10` should be replaced with the hostname for the camera; and the string `video.mjpg` should be replaced with the name of the video stream file.

```
from SimpleCV import JpegStreamCamera

# Initialize the camera with login info in the URL
cam = JpegStreamCamera("http://admin:1234@192.168.1.10/video.mjpg")

cam.getImage().show()
```

 This puts the username and password in plain text in the Python script. Make sure that the Python script is only readable by authorized users.

Notice the formatting of the URL. It takes the form: `http://username:password@host name/MJPG_feed`. For those who have done basic HTTP authentication in the past, this is the same formatting. Once connected, the network camera will work exactly like a local camera.

IP Camera Examples

The classic real world application for an IP camera is a security camera. A WiFi connected web camera can easily stream a live video feed to a central location for monitoring. These examples are focused on basic image capture. Later chapters of the book will talk about how to detect motion and other ideas for creating a more robust application. The two versions of the security camera application are demonstrated:

- Streaming a single live feed
- Capturing multiple streams and displaying them in a single panel

As with the previous examples, these are best run as Python scripts—and not in the SimpleCV shell.

The first example is basic single IP camera. Once configured, it works like a locally connected camera. As a demonstration, the following example shows a feed captured from the IP camera:

```
from SimpleCV import JpegStreamCamera, Display
import time

#initialize the IP camera
cam = JpegStreamCamera("http://35.13.176.227/video.mjpg")  ❶

display = Display()  ❷

img = cam.getImage()
img.save(display)

while not display.isDone():

    img = cam.getImage()
    img.drawText(time.ctime())
    img.save(display)

    # This might be a good spot to also save to disk
    # But watch out for filling up the hard drive

    time.sleep(1)
```

❶ Initialize the IP camera, as described above.

❷ From this point on, the IP camera will work just like other example code described in the previous chapter.

Using Existing Images

The SimpleCV framework does not actually require a physical camera to do image processing. In addition to IP cameras and physically connected cameras, the SimpleCV framework can also process image data previously saved to disk. In other words, a pre-existing video or image can serve as a frame source. This is useful for processing video captured from non-compatible devices or for providing post-processing of previously captured video.

Virtual Cameras

One approach to using existing images is to use a virtual camera. Instead of capturing data fed through a camera, the virtual camera loads a video file that is accessed as though it is a stream of video coming through a camera. By this point in the book, the overall access and use should appear familiar to most readers:

```
from SimpleCV import VirtualCamera

# Load an existing video into the virtual camera
vir = VirtualCamera("chicago.mp4", "video")

vir.getImage().show()
```

The previous example looks for a video named chicago.mp4 as the frame source. The first parameter to VirtualCamera() is the filename of the video to load. The second is simply the word "video," indicating that the first parameter points to a video as opposed to a static image. When working with a virtual camera, each call to getImage() will advance the video by a single frame. Figure 3-3 shows one frame from the example video. Once the last frame of the video is reached, calling getImage() again will loop back to the first frame of the video.

Figure 3-3. Example output from the example video file, opened with the virtual camera

 The ability to use videos as a frame source is based on the codecs installed. The installed codecs will vary from system to system. Under Windows, the video files are decoded with Video for Windows. Linux uses ffmpeg. Mac OS uses QuickTime to decode video files. If in doubt, try to open the file first in another application to see if the video is readable.

Because virtual cameras are based on the Camera class, other camera functionality also works. For example, the Camera.live() function introduced in the previous chapter will work with virtual devices too. Just like with a regular webcam, simply click with the left mouse button on any point on the screen to get information about the pixel coordinates and color. Notice that at the end of the video, it automatically loops back to the beginning and plays it again.

```
from SimpleCV import VirtualCamera

vir = VirtualCamera("chicago.mp4", "video")
```

```
# This plays the video
vir.live()
```

Figure 3-4 shows an example frame from what you would see using this code.

Figure 3-4. Example of the virtual feed using the live() function

Instead of a video file, a single image can also be used as a virtual camera:

```
from SimpleCV import VirtualCamera

# Notice: the second parameter is now: image
vir = VirtualCamera("chicago.png", "image")

vir.getImage().show()
```

This time, the `VirtualCamera` function is passed the path to an image file and then the word "image," indicating that the first parameter is a single image. Because this is only a single image and not a video, `getImage()` always returns the same image. A lot of the same functionality could be achieved by simply loading the image. In fact, the following two lines of code create identical output to the end user:

```
from SimpleCV import Image, VirtualCamera

# These two lines of code do the same thing
VirtualCamera("chicago.png", "image").getImage().show()
Image("chicago.png").show()
```

Notice that the overall functionality of the virtual camera with single images looks a lot like working with the `Image` library. Because the `Image` library also includes additional features to handle drawing and the extraction of features, it is usually the preferred method of working with images.

Examples

The examples provided in this chapter cover a range of applications of image sources. They are designed to demonstrate the range of potential sources and their practical application. The examples cover the following topics:

- Converting a directory of images to the JPEG format
- Using the Kinect to segment an image to extract the nearest object
- Using the Kinect to measure the height of an object
- Combining multiple IP camera feeds into a single feed for easy viewing

Converting Set of Images

This example uses the ImageSet library to convert an entire directory of images to the .jpg format. It first uses the ImageSet to load the directory of images. It then iterates through the set, changing the name of the file to have a .jpg extension. Then it saves the file again with the new file extension and automatically converts it to the new file format during the save process.

```
from SimpleCV import ImageSet

set = ImageSet(".")  ❶

for img in set:  ❷

    oldname = img.filename  ❸

    newname = oldname[0:-3] + 'jpg'  ❹

    print "Converting " + oldname + " to " + newname

    img.save(newname)  ❺
```

❶ The first step is to get an ImageSet of all the files. This example assumes that the code is run from the same directory that contains the images, the Chapter 3 folder. Note that although the *chicago.mp4* file is also in the Chapter 3 folder, it is not an image file, so ImageSet will skip it.

❷ Next, loop over all image files. The img value represents each individual image while looping through the set.

❸ This line extracts the original filename of the image.

❹ This creates the new filename by first finding the name of the original file without the extension (oldname[0:-3]) and then appending the jpg extension.

❺ Finally, save a new copy of the file with the .jpg extension. The .jpg extension will automatically convert the file and save it in the JPEG format.

Segmentation with the Kinect

For the next application, the depth information from the Kinect can be used to extract objects from the foreground and then erase the background. In computer vision, this is known as segmentation, which is the process of dividing an image into groups of related content in order to make the image easier to analyze. Segmentation is covered in greater depth in later chapters, but this example shows how the Kinect can also be used to perform basic segmentation on the image.

 Don't have a Kinect? Example images are provided in the electronic supplement. The 2D image is kinect-image.png and the depth information is stored in kinect-depth.png. Modify the code below to load the images instead of capturing them via the Kinect.

```
from SimpleCV import Kinect
import time

# Initialize the Kinect
kin = Kinect()

# Get the image and depth information
dep = kin.getDepth()    ❶
img = kin.getImage()    ❷

# Turn into a pure black and white image for segmentation
fore = dep.binarize(190).invert()   ❸
fore_only = img - fore   ❹

fore_only.show()   ❺

# Keep the image open for 10 seconds
time.sleep(10)
```

❶ This gets the depth information from the Kinect. The depth information will be used to detect the parts of the image that are in the foreground and the parts that are in the background.

❷ Next, capture an image. This should be done with a still or very slow moving object so that the depth image captured in the previous step matches the picture captured in this step.

❸ This binarizes the depth image, which converts it into a pure black and white image only (no shades of gray). In other words, rather than have many different depths, it will just have foreground and background. The binarization threshold, 190, may need to be adjusted based on the environment. It is then inverted, changing the black to white, and the white to black. By the end of this step, objects in the foreground are black and objects in the background are white.

❹ Subtract the black-and-white image from the main image. This has the effect of removing the background.

❺ Finally, show the resulting image.

The resulting segmentation is not perfect, as you can see in Figure 3-5. It includes a little stuff from right and above the object and misses some material from left and below the object. This is an artifact of the distance between the normal image camera and the depth sensor. Objects farther away from the camera will have less of a problem with this.

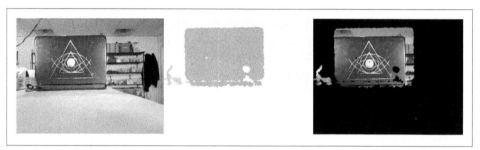

Figure 3-5. Example result of using depth for segmentation. From L–R: The 2D image Center; the depth information; the final result

This is the first of several tricks for extracting important features from an image. It demonstrates how the depth information can be used to reduce the image to only its key components. As the book progresses, we cover these concepts in greater detail, and introduce a variety of different tips and tricks.

Kinect for Measurement

The final Kinect example goes a little further. As demonstrated in the previous example, the 3D depth information is useful for identifying an object of interest because the object of interest is likely closer to the camera than the background objects. This example detects the largest object in the field of view and then tries to measure its height.

```
from SimpleCV import Kinect, Display
import time

# Initialize the Kinect
kin = Kinect()

# Initialize the display
disp = Display((640, 480))  ❶

# This should be adjusted to set how many pixels
# represent an inch in the system's environment
pixelsToInches = 6  ❷

while not disp.isDone():
```

```
img = kin.getDepth()

blobs = img.binarize().findBlobs()  ❸

if (blobs):
    img.drawText(str(blobs[-1].height()/ pixelsToInches) + " inches",
            10, 10)  ❹

img.save(disp)

time.sleep(1)
```

❶ This initializes the display with a specific resolution of 640×480, which matches the output from the Kinect.

❷ This is a calibration value that will need to be adjusted based on the environment in which the code is used. The code will measure how many pixels high an object is, but it needs a way to translate pixels into inches.

❸ Next binarize the image and find blobs. The previous example showed that binarizing the image will help pick out the nearest object. Finding blobs will then look for a big contiguous object, which is assumed to be the object to be measured.

❹ The `drawText()` function should be familiar from Chapter 2. However `blobs[-1].height()` is new. By using `blobs[-1]`, it retrieves the largest blob found. Then it calls `height()` on that blob to get the height in pixels of that object. That measurement is displayed on the screen.

This example requires some calibration. To make it work, start with an object of a known height and place it in front of the camera. Adjust the `pixelsToInches` value until the output shows the correct height in inches. After this calibration is done, the Kinect can be used to measure other objects, such as the laptop in Figure 3-6. The measurements will not be perfect because of limitations in the Kinect sensor, but they should provide a decent estimate of height.

Note, however, that the objects must be put in the same spot as the original object used for calibration. As an extra credit assignment, the depth values could also be calibrated and used to measure physical distance from the camera. This could then be used to measure an object at a more arbitrary distance from the camera—though this is getting more complicated than is appropriate for this early in the book.

Multiple IP Cameras

So far, the security camera examples use only one camera. However, it is common to have multiple security cameras, all of which should be monitored at the same time. The following block of example code shows how to do this by combining the output of four cameras into one display window. This code introduces the `sideBySide()` function, which combines two images together. The options for the `sideBySide()` function in-

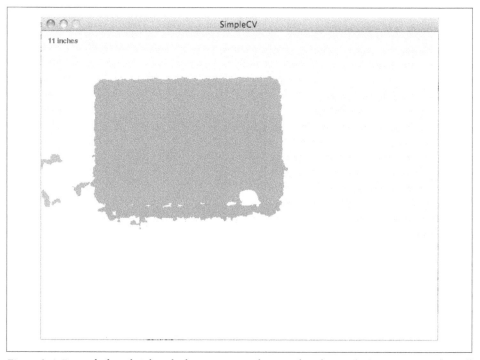

Figure 3-6. Example from height calculator program showing that the nearby laptop is 11 inches tall

clude the name of the image to add to the original image, the side on which place the image (left, right, top, or bottom), and whether or the images should be scaled.

```
from SimpleCV import Camera, Display
import time

#initialize the IP cameras
cam1 = JpegStreamCamera("http://admin:1234@192.168.1.10/video.mjpg")   ❶
cam2 = JpegStreamCamera("http://admin:1234@192.168.1.11/video.mjpg")
cam3 = JpegStreamCamera("http://admin:1234@192.168.1.12/video.mjpg")
cam4 = JpegStreamCamera("http://admin:1234@192.168.1.13/video.mjpg")

display = Display((640,480))   ❷

while not display.isDone():
    img1 = cam1.getImage().resize(320, 240)   ❸
    img2 = cam2.getImage().resize(320, 240)
    img3 = cam3.getImage().resize(320, 240)
    img4 = cam4.getImage().resize(320, 240)

    top = img1.sideBySide(img2)   ❹
    bottom = img3.sideBySide(img4)

    combined = top.sideBySide(bottom, side="bottom")   ❺
```

```
combined.save(display)  ❻
time.sleep(5)
```

❶ Initialize the four IP cameras. Note that each camera has a unique hostname.

❷ Initialize the display at 640×480. This area will support four images, each of size 320×240 to be stacked in a two by two grid.

❸ Capture the image, and then resize to 320×240, so they will all fit into the display.

❹ The sideBySide() function takes two images, and pastes them together side by side into one. First, assemble the top and bottom rows of the grid.

❺ Then take the top and bottom rows of the grid and paste them together into the full grid.

❻ Finally, display the results to the screen, and then sleep for 5 seconds.

An example of what this might look like is shown in Figure 3-7.

Figure 3-7. A display showing the output from multiple security cameras

## CHAPTER 4

Pixels and Images

The previous chapters have provided a broad overview of working with the SimpleCV framework, including how to capture images and display them. Now it is time to start diving into the full breadth of the framework, beginning with a deeper look at images, color, drawing, and an introduction to feature detection. This chapter will drill down to the level of working with individual pixels, and then move up to the higher level of basic image manipulation. Not surprisingly, images are the central object of any vision system. They contain all of the raw material that is then later segmented, extracted, processed, and analyzed. In order to understand how to extract information from images, it is first important to understand the components of a computerized image. In particular, this chapter emphasizes:

- Working with pixels, which are the basic building blocks of images
- Scaling and cropping images to get them to a manageable size
- Rotating and warping images to fit them into their final destination
- Morphing images to accentuate features and reduce noise

Pixels

Pixels are the basic building blocks of a digital image. A pixel is what we call the color or light values that occupy a specific place in an image. Think of an image as a big grid, with each square in the grid containing one color or pixel. This grid is sometimes called a bitmap. An image with a resolution of 1024×768 is a grid with 1,024 columns and 768 rows, which therefore contains 1,024 × 768 = 786,432 pixels. Knowing how many pixels are in an image does not indicate the physical dimensions of the image. That is to say, one pixel does not equate to one millimeter, one micrometer, or one nanometer. Instead, how "large" a pixel is will depend on the pixels per inch (PPI) setting for that image.

Each pixel is represented by a number or a set of numbers—and the range of these numbers is called the color depth or bit depth. In other words, the color depth indicates the maximum number of potential colors that can be used in an image. An 8-bit color depth uses the numbers 0-255 (or an 8-bit byte) for each color channel in a pixel. This means a 1024×768 image with a single channel (black and white) 8-bit color depth would create a 768 kB image. Most images today use 24-bit color or higher, allowing three 0-255 numbers per channel. This increased amount of data about the color of each pixel means a 1024×768 image would take 2.25 MB. As a result of these substantial memory requirements, most image file formats do not store pixel-by-pixel color information. Image files such as GIF, PNG, and JPEG use different forms of compression to more efficiently represent images.

Most pixels come in two flavors: grayscale and color. In a grayscale image, each pixel has only a single value representing the light value, with zero being black and 255 being white. Most color pixels have three values representing red, green, and blue (RGB). Other non-RGB representation schemes exist, but RGB is the most popular format. The three colors are each represented by one byte, or a value from 0 to 255, which indicates the amount of the given color. These are usually combined into an RGB triplet in a (red, green, blue) format. For example, (125, 0, 125) means that the pixel has some red, no green, and some blue, representing a shade of purple. Some other common examples include:

- Red: (255, 0, 0)
- Green: (0, 255, 0)
- Blue: (0, 0, 255)
- Yellow: (255, 255, 0)
- Brown: (165, 42, 42)
- Orange: (255, 165, 0)
- Black: (0, 0, 0)
- White: (255, 255, 255)

Remembering those codes can be somewhat difficult. To simplify this, the Color class includes a host of predefined colors. For example, to use the color teal, rather than needing to know that it is RGB (0, 128, 128), simply use:

```
from SimpleCV import Color

# An easy way to get the RGB triplet values for the color teal.
myPixel = Color.TEAL
```

Similarly, to look up the RGB values for a known color:

```
from SimpleCV import Color

# Prints (0, 128, 128)
print Color.TEAL
```

Notice the convention that all the color names are written in all CAPS. To get green, use Color.GREEN. To get red, use Color.RED. Most of the standard colors are available.

For those readers who would not otherwise guess that Color.PUCE is a built-in color—it's a shade of red—simply type help Color at the SimpleCV shell prompt, and it will list all available colors. Many functions include a color parameter, and color is an important tool for segmenting images. It would be worthwhile to take a moment and review the predefined color codes provided by the SimpleCV framework.

Images

With these preliminaries covered, it is now time to dive into working with images themselves. This section covers how color pixels are assembled into images and how to work with those images inside the SimpleCV framework.

Bitmaps and Pixels

Underneath the hood, an image is a two dimensional array of pixels. A two dimensional array is like a piece of graph paper: there are a set number of vertical units, and a set number of horizontal units. Each square is indexed by a set of two numbers: the first number represents the horizontal row for that square and the second number is the vertical column. Perhaps not surprisingly, the row and columns are indexed by their x and y coordinates.

This approach, called the cartesian coordinate system, should be intuitive based on previous experience with graphs in middle school math courses. However, computer graphics vary from tradition in a very important way. In normal graphing applications, the origin point (0, 0) is in the lower left corner. In computer graphics applications, the (0, 0) point is in the **upper** left corner.

Because the pixels in an image are also in a grid, it's very easy to map pixels to a two-dimensional array. The low-resolution image in Figure 4-1 of a flower demonstrates the indexing of pixels. Notice that pixels are zero indexed, meaning that the upper left corner is at (0, 0) not (1, 1).

The information for an individual pixel can be extracted from an image in the same way an individual element of an array is referenced in Python. The next examples show how to extract the pixel at (120, 150) from the picture of the *Portrait of a Halberdier* painting, as demonstrated in Figure 4-2.

```
from SimpleCV import Image

img = Image('jacopo.png')

# Gets the information for the pixel located at
# x coordinate = 120, and y coordinate = 150
pixel = img[120, 150]

print pixel
```

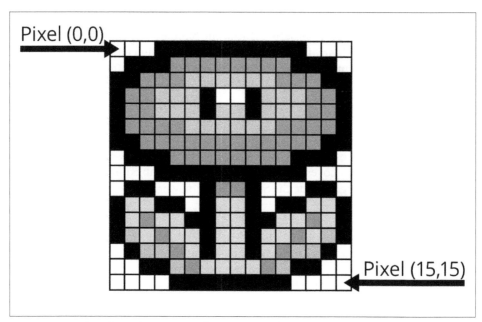

Figure 4-1. Pixels and coordinates. Note that (0, 0) is in the upper-left corner

Figure 4-2. Portrait of a Halberdier by Jacopo Pontormo

The value of `pixel` will become the RGB triplet for the pixel at (120, 150). As a result, `print pixel` returns (242.0, 222.0, 204.0).

The following example code does exactly the same thing, but uses the `getPixel()` function instead of the index of the array. This is the more object-oriented programming approach compared to extracting the pixel directly from the array.

```
from SimpleCV import Image

img = Image('jacopo.png')

# Uses getPixel() to get the information for the pixel located
# at x coordinate = 120, and y coordinate = 150
pixel = img.getPixel(120, 150)

print pixel
```

Want the grayscale value of a pixel in a color image? Rather than converting the whole image to grayscale, and then returning the pixel, use `getGrayPixel(x, y)`.

Accessing pixels by their index can sometimes create problems. In the example above, trying to use `img[1000, 1000]` will throw an error, and `img.getPixel(1000, 1000)` will give a warning because the image is only 300×389. Because the pixel indexes start at zero, not one, the dimensions must be in the range 0-299 on the x-axis and 0-388 on the y-axis. To avoid problems like this, use the `width` and `height` properties of an image to find its dimensions. For example:

```
from SimpleCV import Image

img = Image('jacopo.png')

# Print the pixel height of the image
# Will print 300
print img.height

# Print the pixel width of the image
# Will print 389
print img.width
```

In addition to extracting RGB triplets from an image, it is also possible to change the image using an RGB triplet. The following example will extract a pixel from the image, zero out the green and blue components, preserving only the red value, and then put that back into the image.

```
from SimpleCV import Image

img = Image('jacopo.png')

# Retrieve the RGB triplet from (120, 150)
(red, green, blue) = img.getPixel(120, 150)   ❶
```

```
# Change the color of the pixel+
img[120, 150] = (red, 0, 0)  ❷

img.show()
```

❶ By default, each pixel is returned as a tuple of the red, green, and blue components.
(Chapter 5 covers this in more detail.) This conveniently stores each separate value
in its own variable, appropriately named `red`, `green`, and `blue`.

❷ Now instead of using the original value of green and blue, those are set to zero. Only
the original red value is preserved. This effect is demonstrated in Figure 4-3:

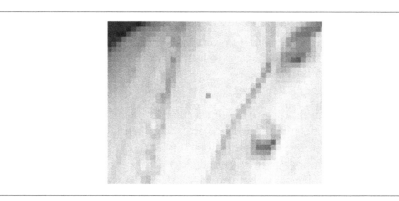

*Figure 4-3. On the left—the image with the new red pixel; on the right—a zoomed view of the changed
pixel*

Since only one pixel was changed, it is hard to see the difference, but now the pixel at
(120, 150) is a dark red color. To make it easier to see, resize the image to five times
its previous size by using the `resize()` function.

```
from SimpleCV import Image

img = Image('jacopo.png')

# Get the pixel and change the color
(red, green, blue) = img.getPixel(120, 150)
img[120, 150] = (red, 0, 0)

# Resize the image so it is 5 times bigger than its original size
bigImg = img.resize(img.width*5, img.height*5)

bigImg.show()
```

The much larger image should make it easier to see the red-only pixel that changed.
Notice, however, that in the process of resizing the image, the single red pixel is interpolated, resulting in extra red in nearby pixels, as demonstrated in Figure 4-4.

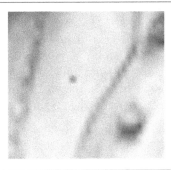

Figure 4-4. The original red pixel after resizing

Right now, this looks like random fun with pixels with no actual purpose. However, pixel extraction is an important tool when trying to find and extract objects of a similar color. Most of these tricks are covered later in the book, but to provide a quick preview of how it is used, the following example looks at the color distance of other pixels compared with a given pixel, as shown in Figure 4-5.

```
from SimpleCV import Image
img = Image('jacopo.png')

# Get the color distance of all pixels compared to (120, 150)
distance = img.colorDistance(img.getPixel(120, 150))

# Show the resulting distances
distance.show()
```

Figure 4-5. Color distance compared to the pixel at (100, 50)

Image Scaling

The block of code above shows the next major concept with images: scaling. In the above example, both the width and the height were changed by taking the `img.height` and `img.width` parameters and multiplying them by 5. In this next case, rather than entering the new dimensions, the `scale()` function will resize the image with just one parameter: the scaling factor. For example, the following code resizes the image to five times its original size.

```
from SimpleCV import Image

img = Image('jacopo.png')

# Scale the image by a factor of 5
bigImg = img.scale(5)

bigImg.show()
```

 Notice that two different functions were used in the previous examples. The `resize()` function takes two arguments representing the new dimensions. The `scale()` function takes just one argument with the scaling factor (how many times bigger or smaller to make the image). When using the `resize()` function and the aspect ratio (the ratio of the width to height) changes, it can result in funny stretches to the picture, as is demonstrated in the next example.

```
from SimpleCV import Image

img = Image('jacopo.png')

# Resize the image, keeping the original height,
# but doubling the width
bigImg = img.resize(img.width * 2, img.height)

bigImg.show()
```

In this example, the image is stretched in the width dimension, but no change is made to the height, as demonstrated in Figure 4-6. To resolve this problem, use adaptive scaling with the `adaptiveScale()` function. It will create a new image with the dimensions requested. However, rather than wrecking the proportions of the original image, it will add padding. For example:

```
from SimpleCV import Image

# Load the image
img = Image('jacopo.png')

# Resize the image, but use the +adaptiveScale()+ function to maintain
# the proportions of the original image
adaptImg = img.adaptiveScale((img.width * 2, img.height))

adaptImg.show()
```

Figure 4-6. The poor Halberdier has gained weight

As you can see in Figure 4-7 in the resulting image, the original proportions are preserved, with the image content placed in the center of the image, and padding is added to the top and bottom of the image.

Figure 4-7. Resized with adaptive scaling

The adaptiveScale() function takes a tuple of the image dimensions, not separate x and y arguments. Hence, the double parentheses.

Adaptive scaling is particularly useful when trying to enforce a standard image size on a collection of heterogeneous images. This example creates 50×50 thumbnail images in a directory called *thumbnails*.

```
from SimpleCV import ImageSet
from os import mkdir

# Create a local directory named thumbnails for storing the images
mkdir("thumbnails")

# Load the files in the current directory
set = ImageSet(".")

for img in set:
    print "Thumbnailing: " + img.filename

    # Scale the image to a +50 x 50+ version of itself,
    # and then save it in the thumbnails folder
    img.adaptiveScale((50, 50)).save("thumbnails/" + img.filename)

print "Done with thumbnails.  Showing slide show."

# Create an image set of all of the thumbnail images
thumbs = ImageSet("./thumbnails/")

# Display the set of thumbnailed images to the user
thumbs.show(3)
```

The adaptiveScale() function has an additional parameter, fit, that defaults to true. When fit is true, the function tries to scale the image as much as possible, while adding padding to ensure proportionality. When fit is false, instead of padding around the image to meet the new dimensions, it instead scales it in such a way that the smallest dimension of the image fits the desired size. Then it will crop the larger dimension so that the resulting image still fits the proportioned size.

A final variant of scaling is the embiggen() function (see Figure 4-8). This changes the size of the image by adding padding to the sides, but does not alter the original image. In some other image editing software, this is the equivalent of changing the canvas size without changing the image. The embiggen() function takes three arguments:

- A tuple with the width and height of the embiggened image.
- The color for the padding to place around the image. By default, this is black.
- A tuple of the position of the original image on the larger canvas. By default, the image is centered.

Figure 4-8. An embiggened image with changed color and position

```
from SimpleCV import Image, Color

img = Image('jacopo.png')

# Embiggen the image, put it on a green background, in the upper right
emb = img.embiggen((350, 400), Color.GREEN, (0, 0))

emb.show()
```

 The embiggen() function will throw a warning if trying to embiggen an image into a smaller set of dimensions. For example, the 300x389 example image cannot be embiggened into a 150×200 image.

Image Cropping

In many image processing applications, only a portion of the image is actually important. For instance, in a security camera application, it may be that only the door—and whether anyone is coming or going—is of interest. Cropping speeds up a program by limiting the processing to a "region of interest" rather than the entire image. The SimpleCV framework has two mechanisms for cropping: the crop() function and Python's slice notation.

Image.crop() takes four arguments that represent the region to be cropped. The first two are the x and y coordinates for the upper left corner of the region to be cropped, and the last two are the width and height of the area to be cropped.

For example, to crop out just the bust in the picture, you could use the following code. The resulting image is shown in Figure 4-9:

```
from SimpleCV import Image

img = Image('jacopo.png')

# Crop starting at +(50, 5)+ for an area 200 pixels wide by 200 pixels tall
cropImg = img.crop(50, 5, 200, 200)

cropImg.show()
```

Figure 4-9. Cropping to just the bust in the image

When performing a crop, it is sometimes more convenient to specify the center of the region of interest rather than the upper left corner. To crop an image from the center, add one more parameter, centered = True, with the result shown in Figure 4-10.

```
from SimpleCV import Image

img = Image('jacopo.png')

# Crop the image starting at the center of the image
cropImg = img.crop(img.width/2, img.height/2, 200, 200, centered=True)

cropImg.show()
```

Figure 4-10. The image cropped around the center

Crop regions can also be defined by image features. Many of these features are covered later in the book, but blobs were briefly introduced in previous chapters. As with other features, the SimpleCV framework can crop around a blob. For example, a blob detection can also find the torso in the picture.

```
from SimpleCV import Image

img = Image('jacopo.png')

blobs = img.findBlobs()  ❶

img.crop(blobs[-1]).show()  ❷
```

❶ This will find the blobs in image.

❷ The findBlobs() function returns the blobs in ascending order by size. This will be covered in greater detail in later chapters. In this example, that means the bust is the largest blob.

Once cropped, the image should look like Figure 4-11.

Figure 4-11. The cropped painting using blobs

The crop function is also implemented for Blob features, so the above code could also be written as follows. Notice that the crop() function is being called directly on the blob object instead of the image object.

```
from SimpleCV import Image

img = Image('jacopo.png')

blobs = img.findBlobs()

# Crop function being called directly on the blob object
blobs[-1].crop().show()
```

Image Slicing

For the Python aficionados, it is also possible to do cropping by directly manipulating the two dimensional array of the image. Individual pixels could be extracted by treating the image like an array and specifying the (x, y) coordinates. Python can also extract ranges of pixels as well. For example, img[start_x:end_x, start_y:end_y] provides a cropped image from (start_x, start_y) to (end_x, end_y). Not including a value for one or more of the coordinates means that the border of the image will be used as the start or end point. So something like img[: , 300:] works. That will select all of the x values and all of the y values that are greater than 300. In essence, any of Python's functions for extracting subsets of arrays will also work to extract parts of an image, and thereby return a new image. Because of this, images can be cropped using Python's slice notation instead of the crop function:

```
from SimpleCV import Image

img = Image('jacopo.png')

# Cropped image that is 200 pixels wide and 200 pixels tall starting at (50, 5).
cropImg = img[50:250,5:205]

cropImg.show()
```

 When using slice notation, specify the start and end locations. When using crop, specify a starting coordinate and a width and height.

Transforming Perspectives: Rotate, Warp, and Shear

When writing a vision application, is is common to assume that the camera is positioned squarely to view an image and that the top of the image is "up." However, sometimes the camera is held at an angle to an object or not oriented squarely to the image. This can complicate the image analysis. Fortunately, sometimes this can be fixed with rotations, shears, and skews.

Spin, Spin, Spin Around

The simplest operation is to rotate the image so that it is correctly oriented. This is accomplished with the rotate() function, which only has one required argument, angle. This value is the angle, in degrees, to rotate the image. Negative values for the angle rotate the image clockwise and positive values rotate it counterclockwise. To rotate the image 45 degrees counterclockwise:

```
from SimpleCV import Image

img = Image('jacopo.png')
```

```
# Rotate the image counter-clockwise 45 degrees
rot = img.rotate(45)

rot.show()
```

The resulting rotated image is shown in Figure 4-12.

Figure 4-12. The image rotated 45 degrees to the left

Generally, rotation means to rotate around the center point. However, a different axis of rotation can be chosen by passing an argument to the point parameter. This parameter is a tuple of the (x, y) coordinate for the new point of rotation.

```
from SimpleCV import Image

img = Image('jacopo.png')

# Rotate the image around the coordinates +(16, 16)+
rot = img.rotate(45, point=(16, 16))

rot.show()
```

The rotated image is shown in Figure 4-13. Notice that the image was cropped during the rotation.

Note that when the image is rotated, if part of the image falls outside the original image dimensions, that section is cropped. The rotate() function has a parameter called fixed to control this. When fixed is set to false, the algorithm will return a resized image, where the size of the image is set to include the whole image after rotation.

For example, to rotate the image without clipping off the corners:

```
from SimpleCV import Image
```

Figure 4-13. Rotation around (16, 16)

```
img = Image('jacopo.png')

# Rotate the image and then resize it so the content isn't cropped
rot = img.rotate(45, fixed=False)

rot.show()
```

The image of the dizzy halberdier is shown in Figure 4-14.

 Even when defining a rotation point, if the `fixed` parameter is false, the image will still be rotated about the center. The additional padding around the image essentially compensates for the alternative rotation point.

Finally, for convenience, the image can be scaled at the same time that it is rotated. This is done with the `scale` parameter. The value of the parameter is a scaling factor, similar to the scale function.

```
from SimpleCV import Image

img = Image('jacopo.png')

# Rotate the image and make it half the size
rot = img.rotate(90, scale=.5)

rot.show()
```

Figure 4-14. Rotation with the canvas resized to fit the whole image

Flipping Images

Similar to rotating, an image can also be flipped across its horizontal or vertical axis (Figure 4-15). This is done with the `flipHorizontal()` and `flipVertical()` functions. To flip the image across its horizontal axis:

```
from SimpleCV import Image

img = Image('jacopo.png')

# Flip the image along the horizontal axis and then display the results
flip = img.flipHorizontal()

flip.show()
```

The following example applies the horizontal flip to make a webcam act like a mirror, perhaps so you can check your hair or apply your makeup with the aid of your laptop.

Figure 4-15. A mirror image of the Jacopo Pontormo painting

```
from SimpleCV import Camera, Display

cam = Camera()

# The image captured is just used to match Display size with the Camera size
disp = Display( (cam.getProperty('width'), cam.getProperty('height')) )

while disp.isNotDone():
    cam.getImage().flipHorizontal().save(disp)
```

Note that a flip is not the same as a rotation by 180 degrees. Figure 4-16 demonstrates the difference between flips and rotations.

Figure 4-16. Left: The original image; Center: The image rotated 180 degrees; Right: The image flipped vertically

Shears and Warps

Images or portions of an image are sometimes skewed to make them fit into another shape. A common example of this is overlaying an image on top of a square object that is viewed at an angle. When viewing a square object at an angle, the corners of the square no longer appear to be 90 degrees. Instead, to align a square object to fit into this angular space, its edges must be adjusted. Underneath the hood, it is performing an affine transformation, though this is more commonly called a shear.

 The tricky part when doing warps is finding all the (x, y) coordinates. Use `Camera.live()` and click on the image to help find the coordinates for the skew.

To demonstrate shearing, the following block of code can be used to fix the Leaning Tower of Pisa (see Figure 4-17). Granted, it makes the other building in the picture tip too far to the left, but some people are never happy.

```
from SimpleCV import Image

img = Image('pisa.png')

corners = [(0, 0), (450, 0), (500, 600), (50, 600)]  ❶

straight = img.shear(corners)  ❷

straight.show()
```

❶ This is a list of the corner points for the sheared image. The original image is 450 x 600 pixels. To fix the tower, the lower right corners are shifted by 50 pixels to the right. Note that the points for the new shape are passed in clockwise order, starting from the top left corner.

❷ Next simply call the **shear()** function, passing the list of new corner points for the image.

Figure 4-17. Left: The original leaning tower; Right: The repaired version of the tower

In addition to shearing, images can also be warped by using the warp() function. Warping also takes an array of corner points as its parameters. Similar to shearing, it is used to stretch an image and fit it into a nonrectangular space.

 A shear will maintain the proportions of the image. As such, sometimes the actual corner points will be adjusted by the algorithm. In contrast, a warp can stretch the image so that it fits into any new shape.

Everybody wants to be on television, but with this next example, now anyone can have the chance to be on TV *and* go back in time. The impudent might even call it a "time warp"...

```
from SimpleCV import Camera, Image, Display

tv_original = Image("family.png")    ❶

tv_coordinates = [(285,  311), (367, 311), (368, 378), (286, 376)]  ❷

tv_mask = Image(tv_original.size()).invert().warp(tv_coordinates)  ❸

tv = tv_original - tv_mask    ❹

cam = Camera()

disp = Display(tv.size())

# While the window is open, keep updating updating
# the TV with images from the camera
while disp.isNotDone():

    bwimage = cam.getImage().grayscale().resize(tv.width, tv.height)  ❺

    on_tv = tv + bwimage.warp(tv_coordinates)    ❻

    on_tv.save(disp)
```

❶ This is the image we'll be using for the background. The image captured via the webcam will be placed on top of the TV.

❷ These are the coordinates of the corners of the television.

❸ Image(tv_original.size()) creates a new image that has the same size as the original TV image. By default, this is an all black image. The invert function makes it white. The warp function then creates a white warped region in the middle, based on the coordinates previously defined for the TV. The result is Figure 4-18.

❹ Using image subtraction, the TV is now removed from the image. This is a trick that will be covered more extensively in the next chapter.

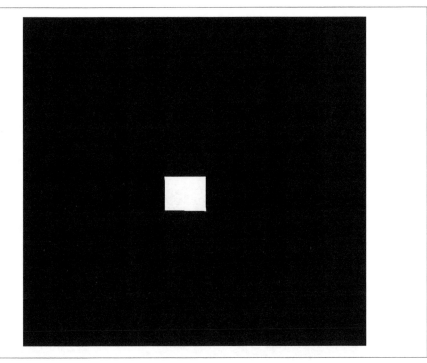

Figure 4-18. The mask for the TV image, which is white where the TV sits and black otherwise

❺ Now capture an image from the camera. To be consistent with the black and white background image, convert it to grayscale. In addition, since this image will be added to the background image, it needs to be resized to match the background image.

❻ Finally, do another warp to make the image from the camera fit into the TV region of the image. This is then added onto the background image (Figure 4-19).

Image Morphology

It is always preferable to control the real-world lighting and environment in order to maximize the quality of an image. However, even in the best of circumstances, an image will include pixel-level noise. That noise can complicate the detection of features on the image, so it is important to clean it up. This is the job of morphology.

Binarization

Many morphology functions work with color images, but they are easiest to see in action when working with a binary (2-color) image. Binary literally means the image is black and white, with no shades of gray. To create a binary image, use the `binarize()` function:

Figure 4-19. Sample output from this example, with our handsome book author appearing on the television

```
from SimpleCV import Image

img = Image('jacopo.png')

imgBin = img.binarize()

imgBin.show()
```

The output is demonstrated in Figure 4-20. Notice that it is purely black and white (no gray).

Whenever an image is binarized, the system needs to know which pixels get converted to black, and which to white. This is called a "threshold", and any pixel where the grayscale value falls under the threshold is changed to white. Any pixel above the threshold is changed to black. By default, the SimpleCV framework uses a technique called Otsu's method to dynamically determine the binarized values. However, the binarize function also takes a parameter value between 0-255. The following example code shows the use of binarization at several levels:

```
from SimpleCV import Image

img = Image('trees.png')
```

Figure 4-20. The Jacopo painting, binarized

```
# Using Otsu's method
otsu = img.binarize()

# Specify a low value
low = img.binarize(75)

# Specify a high value
high = img.binarize(125)

img = img.resize(img.width*.5, img.height*.5)
otsu = otsu.resize(otsu.width*.5, otsu.height*.5)
low = low.resize(low.width*.5, low.height*.5)
high = high.resize(high.width*.5, high.height*.5)


top  = img.sideBySide(otsu)
bottom = low.sideBySide(high)
combined = top.sideBySide(bottom, side="bottom")

combined.show()
```

Figure 4-21 demonstrates the output of these four different thresholds.

Figure 4-21. Top Left: The original imag;e Top Right: Binarized with Otsu's method; Bottom Left: Low threshold value; Bottom Right: High threshold value

Dilation and Erosion

Once the image is converted into a binary format, there are four common morphological operations: dilation, erosion, opening, and closing. Dilation and erosion are conceptually similar. With dilation, any background pixels (black) that are touching an object pixel (white) are turned into a white object pixel. This has the effect of making objects bigger, and merging adjacent objects together. Erosion does the opposite. Any foreground pixels (white) that are touching a background pixel (black) are converted into a black background pixel. This makes the object smaller, potentially breaking large objects into smaller ones.

For the examples in this section, consider the case of a pegboard with tools. The small holes in pegboard can confuse feature detection algorithms. Tricks like morphology can help clean up the image. The first example shows dilating the image. In particular, notice that after binarizing, some of the parts of the tools have disappeared where there was glare. To try to get these back, use dilation to fill in some of the missing parts.

```
from SimpleCV import Image

img = Image('pegboard.png')
```

```
# Binarize the image so that it's a black and white image
imgBin = img.binarize()

# Show the effects of dilate() on the image
imgBin.dilate().show()
```

Notice in Figure 4-22 that although this filled in some of the gaps in the tools, the pegboard holes grew. This is the opposite of the desired effect. To get rid of the holes, use the erode() function.

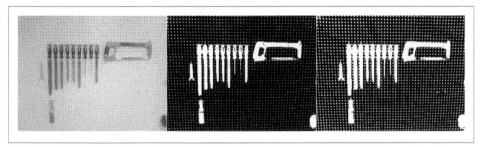

Figure 4-22. Left: The original image Center: Binarized image Right: Dilated image

```
from SimpleCV import Image

img = Image('pegboard.png')

imgBin = img.binarize()

# Like the previous example, but erode()
imgBin.erode().show()
```

As you can see in Figure 4-23, this essentially has the opposite effect. It made a few of the gaps in the image worse, such as with the saw blade. On the other hand, it eliminated most of the holes on the peg board.

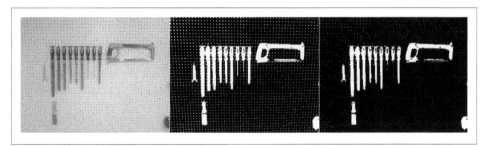

Figure 4-23. Left: The original image; Center: Binarized image; Right: Eroded image

While the dilate() function helps fill in the gaps, it also amplifies some of the noise. In contrast, the erode() function eliminates a bunch of noise, but at the cost of some good data. The solution is to combine these functions together. In fact, the combinations are so common, they have their own named functions: `morphOpen()` and `morphClose()`. The `morphOpen()` function erodes and then dilates the image. The erosion step eliminates very small (noise) objects, following by a dilation which more or less restores the original size objects to where they were before the erosion. This has the effect of removing specks from the image. In contrast, `morphClose()` first dilates and then erodes the image. The dilation first fills in small gaps between objects. If those gaps were small enough, the dilation completely fills them in, so that the subsequent erosion does not reopen the hole. This has the effect of filling in small holes. In both cases, the goal is to reduce the amount of noise in the image.

For example, consider the use of `morphOpen()` on the pegboard. This eliminates a lot of the pegboard holes while still trying to restore some of the damage to the tools created by the erosion, as demonstrated in Figure 4-24.

```
from SimpleCV import Image

img = Image('pegboard.png')

imgBin = img.binarize()

# +morphOpen()+ erodes and then dilates the image
imgBin.morphOpen().show()
```

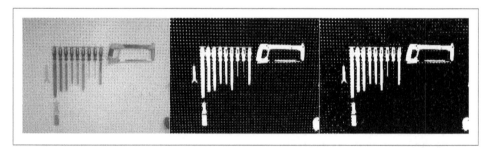

Figure 4-24. Left: The original image; Center: Binarized image; Right: Image after morphOpen()

Although this helped a lot, it still leaves a lot of the pegs in the pegboard. Sometimes, the trick is simply to do multiple erosions followed by multiple dilations. To simplify this process, the `dilate()` and `erode()` functions each take a parameter representing the number of times to repeat the function. For instance, `dilate(5)` performs a dilation five times, as demonstrated in Figure 4-25.

```
from SimpleCV import Image

img = Image('pegboard.png')

# Dilate the image twice to fill in gaps
noPegs = img.dilate(2)

# Then erode the image twice to remove some noise
filled = noPegs.erode(2)
```

```
allThree = img.sideBySide(noPegs.sideBySide(filled))
allThree.scale(.5).show()
```

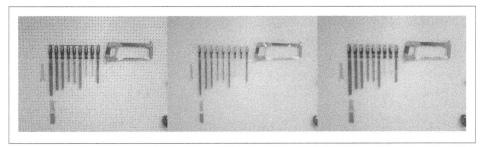

Figure 4-25. Left: The original image; Center: Dilated image; Right: Eroded after dilation

Examples

The examples in this section demonstrate both a fun application and a practical application. On the fun side, it shows how to do a spinning effect with the camera, using the rotate() function. On the practical side, it shows how to shear an object viewed at an angle, and then use the corrected image to perform a basic measurement.

The SpinCam

This is a very simple script which continually rotates the output of the camera. It continuously captures images from the camera. It also progressively increments the angle of rotation, making it appear as though the video feed is spinning.

```
from SimpleCV import Camera

cam = Camera()
display = Display()

# This variable saves the last rotation, and is used
# in the while loop to increment the rotation
rotate = 0

while display.isNotDone():
    rotate = rotate + 5      ❶
    cam.getImage().rotate(rotate).save(display)   ❷
```

❶ Increment the amount of rotation by five degrees. Note that when the rotation exceeds 360 degrees, it automatically loops back around.

❷ Take a new image and rotate by the amount computed in the previous step. Then display the image.

Warp and Measurement

The second example is slightly more practical. Measuring objects is covered in more detail later in this book, but this example provides a general introduction. The basic idea is to compare the object being measured to an object of a known size. For example, if an object is sitting on top of an 8.5×11 inch piece of paper, the relative size of the objects can be used to compute the size. However, this is complicated if the paper is not square to the camera. This example shows how to fix that with the warp() function. The image in Figure 4-26 is used to measure the size of the small building block on the piece of paper.

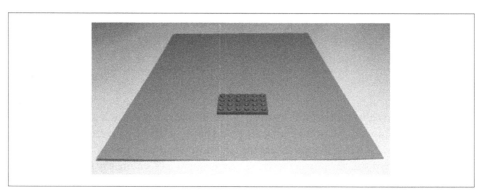

Figure 4-26. The original image of the building block on paper

```
from SimpleCV import Image

img = Image('skew.png')

# Warp the picture to straighten the paper
corners = [(0, 0), (480, 0), (336, 237), (147, 237)]   ❶

warped = img.warp(corners)   ❷

# Find the blob that represents the paper
bgcolor = warped.getPixel(240, 115)

dist = warped.colorDistance(bgcolor)   ❸

blobs = dist.invert().findBlobs()   ❹

paper = blobs[-1].crop()   ❺

# Find the blob that represents the toy
toyBlobs = paper.invert().findBlobs()

toy = toyBlobs[-1].crop()   ❻
```

```
# Use the toy block/paper ratio to compute the size
paperSize = paper.width
toySize = toy.width

print float(toySize) / float(paperSize) * 8.5  ❼
```

❶ These are the coordinates for the four corners of the paper. A good way to help identify the corner points is to use the SimpleCV shell to load the image, and then use the `image.live()` function to display it. Then left-click on the displayed image to find the coordinates of the paper corners.

❷ This warps the image to square the edges of the piece of paper, as shown in Figure 4-27.

❸ Use the `image.live()` trick to also find the color of the paper. This makes it easier to find the part of the image that is the paper versus other background objects. The image below shows the result. Notice that the paper is black whereas the rest of the image is represented in various shades of gray.

❹ By making the paper black, it is easier to pull it out of the image with the `findBlobs()` function.

❺ Next, crop the original image down to just the largest blob (the paper), as represented by `blobs[-1]`. This creates a new image that is just the paper.

❻ Now looking at just the area of the paper, use the `findBlobs` function again to locate the toy block. Create an image of the block by cropping it from off the paper.

❼ Using the ratio of the width of the paper and the toy block, combined with the fact that the paper is 8.5 inches wide, compute the size of the block, which is 1.87435897436, which matches the objects size of 1.875 inches.

Note that this example works best when measuring relatively flat objects. When adjusting the skew, it makes the top of the object appear larger than the bottom, which can result in an over-reported size. Later chapters will discuss blobs in greater depth, including working with blob properties to get a more accurate measurement.

See Figure 4-28 for another example of color distance.

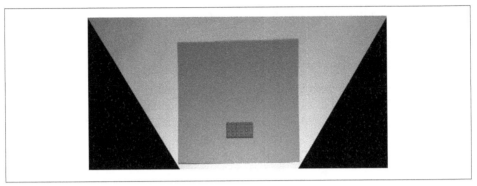

Figure 4-27. The image warped to square the sides of the paper

Figure 4-28. Color distance from the red background, making it easier to extract the paper and the block

The Impact of Light

All vision systems depend on quality images, and quality images in turn depend on light. Because of this, the quality of the light in the vision system environment is a key factor to its success. This chapter takes a deeper look at light and how to use it to illuminate a vision system, including:

- The different types of light sources available
- Ways to evaluate light sources
- Looking at how the target object interacts with light
- Removing unwanted ambient light
- Reviewing different lighting techniques
- Calibrating the camera
- Using color to segment an image

Introduction

One of the most common mistakes of beginning computer vision developers is to overlook lighting and its effect on image quality and algorithm performance. Lighting is a critical component in any vision system and can be the difference between success and failure. After all, without lighting, computer vision would be the study of black rooms with black objects. That would actually make vision programming incredibly easy, but not terribly useful. Instead the lighting should help accomplish three main goals:

- Maximize the contrast of the features of interest
- Be generalized enough that it works well from one object to the next
- Be stable within the environment, particularly over time

Note that in any environment, light radiates from one or more sources and then bounces onto an object (or irradiates it). When filming the object, that surface then radiates the incident light into the camera. It is important to understand this process at an abstract level as it underlies all illumination situations and affects the proposed solutions. A camera does not film the object itself; it films the light reflected from the object (Figure 5-1).

Figure 5-1. Light, camera, action

With lighting, there are three general factors to take into consideration: the source of the light, how the objects being filmed reflect or absorb that light, and how the camera then absorbs and processes the light. It is important to take into account things like the color of the light, the position of the light source in relationship to the target object, and how much of an impact any ambient light might be having on the setup. With the objects, things like the geometry and surface of the object have an impact, as well as its composition and color. If the object's surface is very reflective, that's going to require a different lighting setup than an object whose surface absorbs light instead. Finally, with the camera, consider what the camera is capable of, as well as the best settings to use. At the end of the day, if the sensor in the camera can not utilize the light from the light source, then it's as if the light was not even there in the first place.

Light and the Environment

If possible, it is easier to control the light sources in the environment than it is to write code to compensate for poor lighting. This first section provides some background on the environment, lighting, and other factors that influence the effectiveness of a vision system. It does not involve much sample code, but understanding the environment makes future coding easier. Of course, in some situations, it is not possible to carefully control the environment. For example, outdoor lighting is heavily subject to the weather and time of day. Given these challenges, the next section of this chapter covers how to use the SimpleCV framework to compensate for different lighting situations. But first, some background on creating an environment conducive to machine vision.

Ideally, within the environment, create a situation where the lighting is as consistent and controlled as possible. If there is a lot of light contamination from external light sources, it may help to create an enclosure to block that light. Alternatively, some sources of light can be controlled with filters on the camera. It is even important to consider how the objects themselves will be presented to the camera. Will they be in a consistent location? If they're not going to be in the same location, then a spotlight probably is not the best lighting choice. Will the objects be moving? If they are moving —such as on a conveyor belt—a strobe light might may help to capture the most relevant information. Sometimes a new light source can be added or the light source's orientation can be changed to improve the quality of the image captured. Any changes made to the environment to increase the consistency when filming one object to the next will make the programming easier.

Light Sources

Outside of the environment, there is the source of the light itself. The types of light sources frequently used in vision systems include:

- Fluorescent
- LED
- Quartz Halogen
- Xenon
- Metal Halide
- High Pressure Sodium

When picking a light source, the things to consider are:

- How consistent and reliable they are
- The life expectancy of the bulbs
- How cost effective they might be
- How stable they are, and what the spectrum and intensity is like for the light they emit
- How flexible they are (whether or not they can be adapted for different situations)

Most small to medium sized machine vision applications use either fluorescent, LED, or Quartz Halogen light sources. Fluorescent lighting tends to be very stable, but it does not have as long a life expectancy as other sources. In comparison, LED lighting tends to be stable, adaptable, and has a long life expectancy—but it does not emit as intense a light as a Quartz Halogen source. But the intense light of a Quartz Halogen source also outputs a lot of heat, and does not have a particularly strong life expectancy. Of course, systems are not limited to one type of light source either. They can combine sources to meet whatever the requirements are.

When evaluating light sources, they are generally classified in terms of:

- Brightness, such as a 40 watt light bulb versus a 100 watt light bulb
- Color, such as red and green Christmas lights
- Location, such as overhead lights versus track lighting
- Flavor, such as cloudy days have diffuse lighting, which contrasts to the point source lighting of a sunny day

Most consumer light bulbs use incandescent wattage as an approximation of their brightness, but it is not a very useful measurement. The wattage of a light bulb is the amount of radiant flux, or the total amount of electromagnetic radiation, emitted by the bulb. Electromagnetic radiation includes everything in the infrared, ultraviolet, and visible light spectrum—which also includes thermal radiation, or heat. With the exception of their application for the Easy Bake Oven, the purpose of a light bulb is to emit visible light and not heat. A better way to measure the power of a light is in *lumens* (denoted by the symbol lm). Lumens is the unit of measurement for luminous flux, which is the total amount of visible light emitted by a source. Because most vision systems are only concerned with visible light, it's more useful to use lumens instead of watts when determining lighting specifications.

Another unit of light measurement is *candlepower*, which is often used when rating LEDs. Candlepower is expressed in candelas (cd) or millicandelas (mcd), and is a measurement of the intensity of a light source in a given direction. The relationship between lumens and candelas is that one candela is equal to one lumen per steradian (a steradian being a unit of measurement related to the surface area of a sphere). It is because candelas take into account the directionality of the light that they are useful. Decreasing the beam angle of an LED to give it a tighter focus increases the brightness without actually having to increase the amount of light emitted. In other words, a 1000 mcd LED with a viewing angle of 60 degrees outputs as much total light as a 4000 mcd LED with a viewing angle of 30 degrees—but the 4000 mcd LED will be four times as intense. It's a difference of a factor of four because when cutting the angle in half, the light is cut in two directions for both the width and the height.

The bottom line is that with spotlights, consider the candelas or millicandelas ratings of light sources. With more general lighting, or floodlights, the lumens rating is likely more useful.

Light and Color

The color of a light source is another important consideration when selecting a lighting source. Scientifically speaking, visible light is the part of the electromagnetic spectrum that ranges from low frequency (long wavelength) red light to high frequency (short wavelength) violet light. We use the term *visible light* to talk about the range of the spectrum that humans can see. Different illumination systems generate different colors of light. For example, sunlight at noon is different than a white LED light, which is different than the light of a laser pointer pen. When comparing sources, it is often useful to draw a graph with the rainbow of colors on the x-axis and the amount of light at each color plotted on the y-axis (see Figure 5-2 for an example).

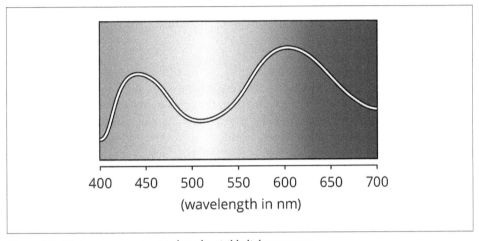

Figure 5-2. Histogram superimposed on the visible light spectrum

One reason that the color of the light is important is that different surfaces respond differently to various colors of light. One example of this effect is an ordinary white t-shirt. When viewing a white t-shirt under most lighting conditions, it appears more or less white. When using a black light, the same shirt can appear to be glowing violet. For any situation where an objects is illuminated by light (regardless of its source), this same effect is in play. This effect can have a significant impact when using color to identify objects and segment images. You can see the impact from different colored light sources in Figure 5-3. If the wrong color light changes the apparent color of the image, the code will fail.

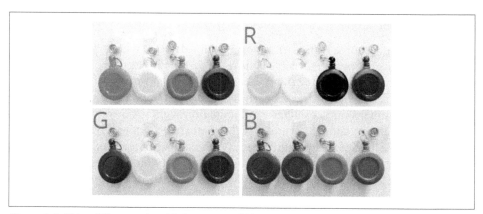

Figure 5-3. Using different colored lights creates different contrasts

Sometimes the color balance of a picture is a bit off, requiring some degree of correction. This is done with a `ColorCurve` object. The color is most simply thought of as a graph where the x-axis is the intensity of the color in the original image and the y-axis is the new intensity. For example, if the curve for the red channel goes through the point (`100`, `120`), then any pixel that had a red value of 100 in the original image will have a value of 120 in the new image. Obviously defining these new values for all 256 possible red values, plus all 256 green values, plus all 256 possible blue values would be a time consuming mess. Instead, `ColorCurve`s are defined with several points, and the rest are interpolated. For example, a curve for the red channel defined by the points (`0`, `0`), (`128`, `128`), and (`256`, `128`) will leave all the low and middle intensity reds untouched, but it will reduce the high intensity reds.

To apply a color curve, first create the `ColorCurve` for each color channel. When working with RGB color, the result is then applied with the `applyRGBCurve()` function. The function takes three arguments: a curve for the R channel, a curve for the G channel, and a curve for the B channel. Curves can also be applied to HSV images with the `applyHSVCurve()` function. It once again takes three arguments of the three curves representing the H, S, and V channels.

The following example demonstrates how to use color curves to apply an old-time photo effect to images from the webcam.

```
from SimpleCV import Camera, Display, ColorCurve, Image

screenSize = (640, 480)

rCurve = ColorCurve([[0,0],[64,64],[128,128],[256,128]])  ❶

gbCurve = ColorCurve([[0,16],[64,72],[128,148],[256,256]])  ❷

cam = Camera(-1, {'width': screenSize[0], 'height': screenSize[1]} )

disp = Display(screenSize)
```

```
while not disp.isDone():
    img = cam.getImage()

    coloredImg = img.applyRGBCurve(rCurve, gbCurve, gbCurve)  ❸

    erodedImg = coloredImg.erode(1)  ❹

    erodedImg.save(disp)
```

❶ The first curve will be used for the red channel. It reduces the high intensity red colors.

❷ The second curve will be used for the green and blue channels. It provides a slight boost to the mid-level green and blue channels.

❸ Apply the curve to the image. Note that rCurve is used for just the red channel, whereas gbCurve is passed both for the green and blue channels.

❹ Adding an erode to the image provides a little additional old-time photo look to the image.

The Target Object

While the brightness and color refer to the light source, the nature of the object itself also affects how light interacts with it. When light reflects off of an object, it always follows the law of reflection, which states that the angle at which the light approached the object (the incident ray) is the same angle at which the light will leave the object (the reflected ray). When an object's surface is completely smooth, as in the case of a mirror, then all of the incoming light will be reflected uniformly away from the object. This is known as a specular reflection and will make the object seem shiny because of all of the reflected light. However, if the surface of the object is not smooth, such as with a piece of paper, then the incoming light hits the varied surface at different angles —and because it still obeys the law of reflection, the reflected light then leaves the object using those same angles. Because the light rays are not leaving the object in a uniform manner, the light is scattered and the object appears to have more of a dull finish. This is known as a diffused reflection (see Figure 5-4).

The nature of an object, or what it consists of, impacts more then just how smooth its surface is. Some materials absorb light; some transmit the light and let it shine right through. Some materials are fluorescent and when they absorb light at one wavelength, may emit light at a different wavelength. Then there's also the geometry of the object; a curved surface is going to reflect light differently than a flat one. One of the easiest ways to deal with all of these considerations is a simple trial and error process to test how various light sources interact with a sample object. Because the lighting can have such a dramatic impact on the image quality, it's a good idea to do this early in the process of developing a vision system.

The following terms are sometimes used when describing the surface of an object:

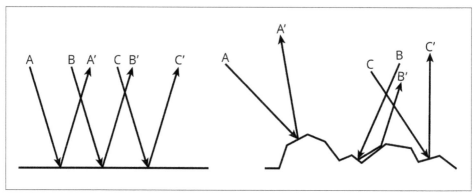

Figure 5-4. How a rough surface diffuses light

Lambertian

Normal or matte surfaces. Light reflects predictably off the object, based only on the position of the light source. Examples include terra cotta, unfinished wood, paper, and fabric. These types of objects are among the easiest to capture with computer vision and are the most robust under different lighting considerations. An example image is shown in Figure 5-5.

Sub-surface scattering

Light penetrates the objects, interacts with the material, and exits at another point. Examples include milk, skin, bone, shells, wax, and marble. The position of the source of light can sometimes have unpredictable results, making it important to plan lighting carefully and have consistent lighting to ensure high quality results. An example is shown in Figure 5-6.

Specular

Shiny objects, such as polished metals, glass, and mirrors. These objects are difficult to use in computer vision systems because their surfaces may include reflections on other objects from their surroundings. When dealing with smooth specular surfaces, it is common to have lighting in a specific pattern and analyze the reflection, rather than the object itself. An example is demonstrated in Figure 5-7.

Figure 5-5. The Terracotta Army, a lambertian surface

Figure 5-6. Sub-surface scattering through wax

Figure 5-7. A glass sculpture with a specular surface

Albedo

A measure of of the percentage of light reflected by an object. Albedo is measured from zero to one, with one meaning that 100% of the light directed on to the object is then reflected. Objects with a higher albedo look more white. Objects with a lower albedo appear darker, as they absorb most of the light that hits them. This determines the quantity of light that usable in an application. An example is shown in Figure 5-8.

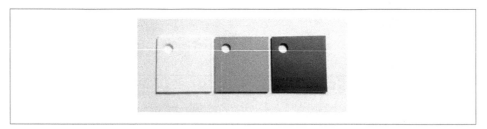

Figure 5-8. The albedo effect

Besides strength and color, light is also classified according to *point-source*, *diffuse*, and *ambient* light. A point source light is basically a light bulb or the sun. A diffuse source is light that has been diffused though another object, such as clouds or a diffuser attached to a camera flash. Ambient lighting is a catch-all term for light that has bounced off multiple objects before the object of interest.

Lighting Techniques

The final area to consider is the lighting techniques. The following is a quick outline of some of the more popular techniques:

Technique	Lighting Type & Direction	Advantages	Disadvantages	Example
Diffuse Dome Lighting	Diffused light source, placed in front of the object	Effective at lighting curved, specular surfaces	Usually requires close proximity to the object	
Diffuse On Axis Lighting	Diffused light source, placed in front of the object	Effective at lighting flat, specular surfaces	Usually requires close proximity to the object	
Bright Field Lighting	A point light source, placed in front of the object	The most commonly used lighting technique. It's good for enhancing topographical details.	With specular or curved surfaces, it can create strong reflections	
Dark Field Lighting	A point light source, placed at the side of the object	Good for finding surface imperfections	Does not illuminate flat, smooth surfaces	
Diffuse Backlighting	A diffuse light source, placed behind the object	Creates a high-contrast silhouette of an object; useful for finding the presence of holes or gaps	The edges of the silhouette may be fuzzy	
Collimated Backlighting	A point light source, placed behind the object	Creates sharp edges on a silhouette, so good for measuring the overall dimensions of an object	Not good for recording topographical details	

Color

In addition to the illumination, it is also important to understand the color of the image. Although color sounds like a relatively straightforward concept, different representations of color are useful in different contexts. The following examples work with an image of *The Starry Night* by Vincent van Gogh, as shown in Figure 5-9.

Figure 5-9. The Starry Night, used in the examples that follow

In the SimpleCV framework, the colors of an individual pixel are extracted with the `getPixel()` function. This was previously demonstrated in Chapter 4.

```
from SimpleCV import Image

img = Image('starry_night.png')

print img.getPixel(0, 0)  ❶
```

❶ Prints the RGB triplet for the pixel at (0,0), which will equal (71.0, 65.0, 54.0).

One criticism of RGB is that it does not specifically model luminance. Yet the luminance/brightness is one of the most common properties to manipulate. In theory, the luminance is the relationship of the of R, G, and B values. In practice, however, it is sometimes more convenient to separate the color values from the luminance values. For example, the difference between a bright yellow and a dark yellow is non-intuitively controlled by the amount of blue. The solution is HSV, which stands for hue, saturation, and value. The color is defined according to the hue and saturation, while value is the measure of the luminance/brightness. The HSV color space is essentially just a transformation of the RGB color space because all colors in the RGB space have a corresponding unique color in the HSV space, and vice versa. It is easy to convert images between the RGB and HSV color spaces, as is demonstrated below.

```
from SimpleCV import Image

img = Image('starry_night.png')

hsv = img.toHSV()   ❶

print hsv.getPixel(25,25)   ❷

rgb = hsv.toRGB()   ❸

print rgb.getPixel(25,25)   ❹
```

❶ This converts the image from the original RGB to HSV.

❷ In this first print statement, since the image was converted to HSV, it will print the HSV values for the pixel at (25,25). In this case, those are (117.0, 178.0, 70.0).

❸ This line converts the image back to RGB.

❹ This will now print the RGB triplet (21.0, 26.0, 70.0).

The HSV color space is particularly useful when dealing with an object that has a lot of specular highlights or reflections. In the HSV color space, specular reflections will have a high luminance value (V) and a lower saturation (S) component. The hue (H) component may get noisy depending on how bright the reflection is, but an object of solid color will have largely the same hue even under variable lighting. We'll look at hue segmentation further in Chapter 8.

Grayscale is the final color encoding scheme commonly used in programs developed with the SimpleCV framework. A grayscale image represents the luminance of the image, but lacks any color components. It is often referred to as a black-and-white image, though it is important to understand the difference between a grayscale and a binary black-and-white image. In the later case, there are only two values: 0 and 1 for pure black and pure white, respectively. In contrast, an 8-bit grayscale image has many shades of grey, usually on a scale from 0 to 255. The challenge is to create a single value from 0 to 255 out of the three values of red, green, and blue found in an RGB image. There is no single scheme for doing this, but it is done by taking a weighted average of the three. To create a grayscale image:

```
from SimpleCV import Image

img = Image('starry_night.png')

gray = img.grayscale()   ❶

print gray.getPixel(0,0)   ❷
```

❶ This converts the image to a grayscale image. The result in shown in Figure 5-10.

❷ This prints the grayscale value for the pixel at (0,0), with the result of (66.0, 66.0, 66.0).

Figure 5-10. The Starry Night, converted to grayscale

Notice that it returns the same number three times. This keeps a consistent format with RGB and HSV, which both return three values. However, since grayscale only has one value, representing the luminance, the same value is repeated three times. To get the grayscale value for a particular pixel without having to convert the image to grayscale, use getGrayPixel().

Color and Segmentation

Chapter 3 introduced the concept of segmentation, which is the process of dividing an image into areas of related content. These areas consist of pixels that all share a particular characteristic, and one of the more frequently used characteristics is color. It is easy to use color to segment an image. This technique is very effective when a color of the desired object is substantially different from the background color, such as tracking a brightly colored object such as a ball. In this case, use the color difference to segment the image and remove the background from the image, leaving just the object of interest.

This works by essentially subtracting one image from another. To understand this, first consider how subtraction works with pixels (a topic which is covered more extensively in the next chapter). Assume that the pixel at point (0, 0) is purple, with the RGB triplet (100, 0, 100). Take an identical pixel—(100, 0, 100)—and subtract it from the original pixel. To do this, simply subtract each element from its corresponding value. (100, 0, 100) - (100, 0, 100) = (0, 0, 0). Since (0, 0, 0) is the RGB value for black, subtracting the same RGB value from a pixel results in a black pixel. Different

colored pixels can also be subtracted from each other. For example, (100, 0, 100) -
(90, 0, 10) = (10, 0, 90), which results in a mostly blue pixel. Subtracting images is
just like subtracting pixels, with the system going through the image on a pixel-by-pixel
basis and performing the subtraction for each pixel.

Color segmentation is based on subtracting away the pixels that are far away from the
target color, while preserving the pixels that are similar to the color. This requires
measuring all of the colors involved to gauge how far away they are from the target
color. The Image class has a function called colorDistance() that computes the distance
between every pixel in an image and a given color. This function takes as an argument
the RGB value of the target color, and it returns another image representing the distance
from the specified color. This is perhaps easier to understand by looking at an example,
so let's work with a picture of a yellow glue gun, as seen in Figure 5-11.

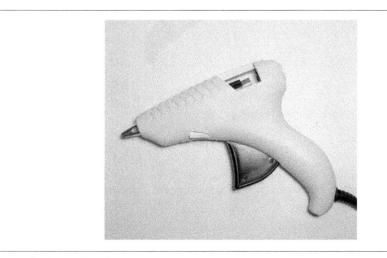

Figure 5-11. A yellow glue gun

```
from SimpleCV import Image, Color

yellowTool = Image("yellowtool.png")

yellowDist = yellowTool.colorDistance((223, 191, 29))  ❶

yellowDistBin = yellowDist.binarize(50).invert()  ❷

yellowDistBin.show()
```

❶ The first step is to find the RGB values for the target color. In this example, the RGB
triplet of (100, 75, 125) is the approximate value for the yellow of the glue gun.
Passing this RGB value into the colorDistance function causes the function return
a grayscale image, where colors close to yellow are black and colors far away from
yellow are white.

❷ Some of the pixels in the background are yellow as well. Since we're not interested in these pixels, we filter some of them out with the `binarize()` function. Recall that the `binarize` function turns the grayscale image into a strictly black and white one. By passing it a threshold value of 50, `binarize` will turn any pixel with a grayscale value under 50 to white, while all other pixels will be turned black.

The resulting image should look like Figure 5-12.

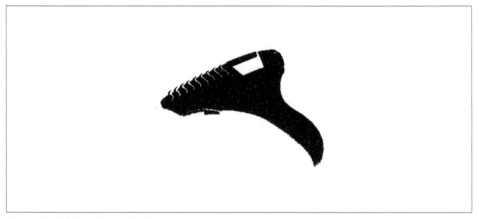

Figure 5-12. The yellow color distance

 There is still a little noise in the image. Use functions like `erode()` and `morphOpen()`, which were covered in the previous chapter, to clean up the noise.

Now the distance image can be subtracted from the original image to remove any portions of the image that are not yellow.

```
from SimpleCV import Image, Color

yellowTool = Image("yellowtool.png")

yellowDist = yellowTool.colorDistance((223, 191, 29))

yellowDistBin = yellowDist.binarize(50).invert()

onlyYellow = yellowTool - yellowDistBin

onlyYellow.show()
```

This will result in an image with only the yellow body of the tool and everything else blacked out, as shown in Figure 5-13.

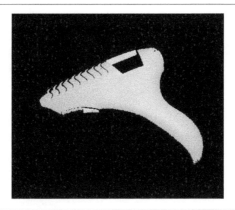

Figure 5-13. Only the yellow body of the tool remains

Example

Let's walk through an example where we detect if a car is illegally parked in a handicap parking space. At the Sight Machine offices, there is a repeat offender who drives a yellow car, parks illegally, and does not have a handicap sticker. Figure 5-14 shows what the image looks like without the car in the spot.

Figure 5-14. The parking lot at the Sight Machine offices

Figure 5-15 shows the offending car in the handicap parking spot.

Example | 97

Figure 5-15. The offending car parked illegally in the handicap parking spot

A simple test would be to simply look for yellow in the image. However, if the yellow car is parked adjacent to the handicap spot, then there is no violation. Instead, this "yellow detector" vision system will have to look whether yellow appears in a particular area in the image.

First, load the images of the car:

```
from SimpleCV import Image

car_in_lot = Image("parking-car.png")    ❶

car_not_in_lot = Image("parking-no-car.png")   ❷
```

❶ Loads the image of the yellow car in the parking space.

❷ Loads the image of the empty parking space.

The next step is to use the picture of the car in the spot to determine the area to inspect. Since the original image contains both acceptable and illegal parking spaces, it needs to be cropped to cover only the handicap space. The whole image is 800×600 pixels. The location of the handicap space is the box around the car, sometimes referred to as the Region of Interest (ROI). In this case, the ROI starts at (470, 200) and is about 200×200 pixels.

```
from SimpleCV import Image

car_in_lot = Image("parking-car.png")

car_not_in_lot = Image("parking-no-car.png")

car = car_in_lot.crop(470,200,200,200)  ❶

# Show the results
car.show()
```

❶ Crops the image to just the area around the car in the parking space.

The resulting picture should look like Figure 5-16.

Figure 5-16. The cropped image

Now that the image is narrowed down to only the handicap spot, the next step is to find the car in the image. The general approach is similar to the yellow glue gun example given earlier. First, find the pixels that are near yellow:

```
from SimpleCV import Image

car_in_lot = Image("parking-car.png")

car_not_in_lot = Image("parking-no-car.png")

car = car_in_lot.crop(470,200,200,200)

yellow_car = car.colorDistance(Color.YELLOW)  ❶

# Show the results
yellow_car.show()
```

❶ This returns a grayscale image showing how far away from yellow all of the colors are in the image.

The resulting image should look like Figure 5-17.

Example | 99

Figure 5-17. The color distances away from yellow

With the color distances computed, subtract out the other colors, leaving only yellow components. This should result in just the car, subtracting out the rest of the image.

```
from SimpleCV import Image

car_in_lot = Image("parking-car.png")

car_not_in_lot = Image("parking-no-car.png")

car = car_in_lot.crop(470,200,200,200)

yellow_car = car.colorDistance(Color.YELLOW)

only_car = car - yellow_car  ❶

# Show the results
only_car.show()
```

❶ Subtracts the grayscale image from the cropped image to get an image of just the yellow car.

As expected, only the car remains, as shown in Figure 5-18.

Figure 5-18. The yellow of the car

To compare this to images that do not have the yellow car in them, there must be some sort of metric to represent the car. One simple way to do this is with the meanColor() function. As the name implies, this computes the average color for the image:

```
from SimpleCV import Image

car_in_lot = Image("parking-car.png")

car_not_in_lot = Image("parking-no-car.png")

car = car_in_lot.crop(470,200,200,200)

yellow_car = car.colorDistance(Color.YELLOW)

only_car = car - yellow_car

print only_car.meanColor()   ❶
```

❶ This prints out what the mean color value is. The result should be: (25.604575, 18.880775, 4.482825).

This is the metric for the space when occupied by the yellow car. Repeat the process for the empty place.

```
from SimpleCV import Image

car_in_lot = Image("parking-car.png")

car_not_in_lot = Image("parking-no-car.png")

car = car_in_lot.crop(470,200,200,200)

yellow_car = car.colorDistance(Color.YELLOW)

only_car = car - yellow_car

no_car = car_not_in_lot.crop(470,200,200,200)

without_yellow_car = no_car.colorDistance(Color.YELLOW)   ❶

# Show the results
without_yellow_car.show()
```

❶ Returns a grayscale image showing how far away from yellow the colors are in the empty space.

Notice in Figure 5-19 that this essentially creates an "empty" image.

Example | 101

Figure 5-19. The color distance away from yellow when the car is not present

Once again, subtract the color distance image and compute the mean color:

```
from SimpleCV import Image

car_in_lot = Image("parking-car.png")

car_not_in_lot = Image("parking-no-car.png")

car = car_in_lot.crop(470,200,200,200)

yellow_car = car.colorDistance(Color.YELLOW)

only_car = car - yellow_car

no_car = car_not_in_lot.crop(470,200,200,200)

without_yellow_car = no_car.colorDistance(Color.YELLOW)

only_space = no_car - without_yellow_car

print only_space.meanColor()
```

The resulting mean color will be: (5.031350000000001, 3.6336250000000003, 4.683625). This contrasts substantially with the mean color when the car is in the image, which was (25.604575, 18.880775, 4.4940750000000005). The amount of blue is similar, but there is substantially more red and green when the car is in the image. This should sound right given that yellow is created by combining red and green.

Given this information, it should be relatively easy to define the thresholds for determining if the car is in the lot. For example, something like the following should do the trick:

```
from SimpleCV import Image

car_in_lot = Image("parking-car.png")

car_not_in_lot = Image("parking-no-car.png")

car = car_in_lot.crop(470,200,200,200)
```

```
yellow_car = car.colorDistance(Color.YELLOW)

only_car = car - yellow_car

(r, g, b) = only_car.meanColor()

if ((r > 15) and (g > 10)):   ❶
    print "The car is in the lot.  Call the attendant."
```

❶ If the red and green values are high enough, the yellow car is probably in the parking space.

In cases where there is enough yellow—as defined by enough red and green—it indicates that the violating car is in the lot. If not, it does nothing. Note that this prints the message for any yellow car in the parking space, as well as any other large, yellow object. Of course this is just a basic example, it could be refined by matching other objects of the car, such as its shape or size.

Example | 103

## CHAPTER 6

Image Arithmetic

As discussed in Chapters 3 and 4, we can think of images as a grid of pixels with each pixel having a color defined as an RGB triplet. Each component in that RGB triplet has a value in the range of 0 to 255. Given this structure and format, it is actually quite easy to perform arithmetic on images, such as addition, subtraction, multiplication, and division. This concept should not be entirely new. Chapter 5 already introduced this idea when using color to segment images. The goal of this section is to examine this concept in further detail, and understand how mathematical manipulation of images is used in a vision system. Topics include:

- The basic mathematical operations from elementary school, as applied to images
- Using histograms to calibrate the camera
- Finding the dominant colors of an image and using that information to segment the image

Basic Arithmetic

Just as with elementary school arithmetic, the easiest place to start is with addition. Two images can be added together. Underneath the hood, the SimpleCV framework goes through the two images pixel by pixel, and adds the RGB values of the pixels at corresponding locations together. Starting at pixel (0,0) on both images (the top left corner of each image), it will add the values for each component of the RGB triplet together to get a new RGB triplet. For instance, if the RGB value of the pixel at (0,0) in the first image is (1,2,3), and the RGB value at the same (0,0) point in the second image is (4,5,6), then when the RGB values are added together, the result would be (5,7,9). This would then be the RGB triplet for the pixel at (0,0) in the resulting image. If the sum of two of the RGB components exceeds the maximum value of 255, then the value for the resulting image is capped at 255. This is tedious work by hand, but it is a case where computer vision shines. An example is shown below:

```
from SimpleCV import Image
```

```
imgA = Image("starry_night.png")


# Add the image to itself
added = imgA + imgA

added.show()
```

Figure 6-1 shows the results of this addition. It looks quite similar to the original image. The most obvious difference is that the image became a lot brighter. Because the maximum value for an RGB component is 255, the "maximum" color is then the one represented by the RGB triplet (255, 255, 255), which is white. This means that adding any two pixels together always brings them closer to white, resulting in a brighter image. The pixels that were already white—or close to white—had relatively little change. On the other end of the spectrum, the dark pixels also did not change much. For example, part of the edge line around the church has a color of (36, 31, 27). Doubling this only provides (72, 62, 54), which is still a pretty dark color.

Figure 6-1. Left: The original image; Right: After the image was added to itself

Adding an image to itself should conjure up thoughts of the next possible operation. Technically adding an image to itself is the same as multiplying it by two. This has the same effect:

```
from SimpleCV import Image

imgA = Image("starry_night.png")

# Double the value of each pixel
mult = imgA * 2

mult.show()
```

Image multiplication is handy when trying to brighten an image. Although the above example is no different than simply adding the image to itself, multiplication is more flexible in an important way. An image can be multiplied by fractions, such as `mult = imgA * 1.5`. For an image that needs a lot of brightening, multiplying by larger numbers is an easy way to brighten it.

```
from SimpleCV import Image

imgA = Image("starry_night.png")

# Double the value of each pixel
mult = imgA * 1.5

mult.show()
```

 With the exception of regions that are pure black (0, 0, 0), multiplying an image by a large number eventually results in a white image.

The resulting picture will look like Figure 6-2. Notice that unlike simply adding the image to itself, this brightened the image without blowing out the white/light portions of the image. It provides a finer degree of control over the brightening process. However, this approach is not perfect. In many photographs, brightening an image also amplifies the background noise, which results in a grainy image.

Figure 6-2. Left: The original image; Right: After the image was brightened using image multiplication

Subtraction was first introduced in Chapter 4, and then revisited in Chapter 5. However, it can be used for more than just segmenting an image with color. In fact, the examples at the end of this chapter show how important subtraction is for tricks like green screening. The first and most basic example is subtracting an image from itself:

```
from SimpleCV import Image

logo = Image("starry_night.png")
```

```
# Subtract an image from itself
# Resulting in a blank image
sub = logo - logo

sub.show()
```

OK, that is a really silly example. It just creates a black image, as demonstrated in Figure 6-3.

Figure 6-3. The most exciting image in the book: subtracting an image from itself

 When subtracting, pixels cannot have an RGB component with a value of less than zero. Negative values are converted to zeros.

After all, any number minus itself is zero. Just as in general arithmetic, subtraction is useful for finding the difference between two things. The difference between two of the exact same things is zero, which is pure black in the world of images. However, it also is a very practical way to check if anything changed between two points in time. For example, assume that a hypothetical book author has been raiding the candy jar instead of writing. A simple application could detect if the candy jar has been moved between two points in time. Notice what happens in the case below:

```
from SimpleCV import Image

# Load the pictures from time A and time B
timeA = Image("candyA.png")
timeB = Image("candyB.png")

# Compare the images by subtracting
diff = timeA - timeB

# The little marks on the image indicate the images are slightly different
diff.show()
```

If the jar was not moved, then the two images should be identical (assuming no change in ambient lighting conditions, and so on). Based on a casual look at the two images, the candy jar looks pretty similar in both. Obviously, if someone was sneaking candy, they were pretty careful about the placement. However, when looking at the results of the subtraction in the example (see Figure 6-4), there is an obvious artifact both from the jar being moved and from the candy in the jar being rustled around. This is another case where computer vision excels. People are not good at noticing very small changes over time. Computers can detect those types of changes easily.

Figure 6-4. Left: Candy jar at time 1; Center: Candy jar at time 2; Right: Difference between images

The above example can be further expanded. For example, this still requires a human to watch the output and determine if the image changes. An even better system would automate the process, looking for changes, and create a notice when the jar was moved. One possible automation approach is to check if more than 10% of the pixels changed.

```
from SimpleCV import Image

# Take the candy difference computed in the previous example
diff = Image("candydiff.png")

# Extract the individual pixels into a flat matrix
matrix = diff.getNumpy()     ❶
flat = matrix.flatten()      ❷

# Find how much changed
num_change = np.count_nonzero(flat)                        ❸
percent_change = float(num_change) / float(len(flat))      ❹
```

```
if percent_change > 0.1:  ❺
    print "Stop eating candy!"
```

❶ An image is essentially just a matrix of pixel values. Therefore, to apply mathematical techniques to an image, it is sometimes easier to have it in a matrix format. The getNumpy() function returns a NumPy matrix of the image.

❷ The NumPy matrix is actually a three dimensional matrix with the dimensions 640×480×3. This corresponds to the 640×480 image dimensions, with an additional dimension for the three values for red, green, and blue. However, rather than looping over a three dimensional array, it will be easier to flatten this into a 921,600×1 array.

❸ We can use Numpy (imported by default in the SimpleCV framework as "np") to quickly count the number of non-zero pixels.

❹ Compute the percentage of values that changed. Recall that num_change is the counter of the number of pixels that are not black, indicating a difference in the image. The len(flat) computes the size of the total number of pixels in the image (or more accurately, in the flattened matrix that represents the image).

❺ Finally, check if the number of pixels changed exceeds the threshold (10%). If it does, print out a warning. In this case, around 22% of the pixels changed, which triggers the message.

> The meanColor() function introduced in the previous chapter would be another way to detect a change. If the images are the same, the mean color is black. Otherwise, the differences have different colors, which impact the value of the mean color. Of course, for minor changes, the differences in the mean color are minimal. Once again, setting an appropriate threshold for the difference in mean color values helps manage the false positive or negative alerts.

The final piece of image arithmetic to cover is division. This is useful when adjusting the contrast. This would be a good time to note that multiplying and then dividing an image by the same number does not necessarily return the image to its original state. For example:

```
from SimpleCV import Image

img = Image('starry_night.png')

mult = img * 2
div = mult / 2

div.show()
```

Elementary school mathematics might suggest that multiplying an image by two and then dividing it by two would restore the image to its original state. Yet the results demonstrated in Figure 6-5 contradict this. Notice that some of the yellows in the

Figure 6-5. Left: The original image; Center: After multiplying by 2; Right: Dividing the multiplied image

original image are turned into white after multiplying. Then they become a shade of gray after dividing. The reason is because of that maximum value of 255 for any given RGB component. During the multiplication process, some of the RGB values are capped at 255. When they are subsequently divided by two, they get a value of 127. For example, if a pixel starts with a red value of 166, multiplying it by two would be 332, which is capped to the maximum value of 255. Dividing that by two results in 127 instead of 166. As a result, chains of mathematical operations on images may create unexpected results. The order of operations can, therefore, be very important.

In general, any operation that can be performed on a NumPy matrix can also be done on an image. Computations like averages (means) and standard deviations are particularly useful. The example below is a basic security camera application that looks for movement or change in the image. Because it is trying to capture a nearly continuous feed of images, speed is much more important. Hence, relying on the mean() function in NumPy is a much more efficient approach than the previous candy jar example.

```
from SimpleCV import Camera, Display
import time

# if mean color exceeds this amount, do something
threshold = 5.0

cam = Camera()
previous = cam.getImage()

disp = Display(previous.size())

while not disp.isDone():
    # Grab another frame and compare with previous
    current = cam.getImage()
    diff = current - previous

    # Convert to NumPy matrix and compute mean color
    matrix = diff.getNumpy()
    mean = matrix.mean()

    # Show on screen
```

```
diff.save(disp)


# Check if changed
if mean >= threshold:
    print "Motion Detected"

# Wait for one second
time.sleep(1)
previous = current
```

 In this example, the threshold represents the mean color, not the percent of pixels that changed.

Histograms

Another useful tool when performing mathematical calculations on images is to use a histogram. In a non-vision sense, histograms are commonly used in statistics to plot the values in a list. They are used to graphically identify frequently or infrequently occurring items. In the world of computer vision, histograms are typically used for listing the colors from each color channel in an image. This is sometimes known as a color channel histogram. This is helpful when manipulating the color and brightness of an image.

The simplest color channel histogram is with a grayscale image. Each pixel in a grayscale image only has one value representing the brightness of that pixel (or what shade of gray it is)—as opposed to the three values representing the different color values in an RGB image. Each of these grayscale values will be in the range from 0 to 255, with 0 being black and 255 being white. To view the brightness histogram of *The Starry Night*:

```
from SimpleCV import Image

img = Image('starry_night.png')

# Generate the histogram
histogram = img.histogram()

# Output the raw histogram data
print histogram
```

This code example outputs a list of 50 values. Each value is the number of pixels that occur at each level of brightness. But wait, why were 50 values outputted when there are 256 shades of gray? The `histogram()` function divides the dataset into bins that combine values from the x-axis of the chart. This has a tendency to smooth out the chart by grouping levels together. However, the number of bins is customizable.

```
from SimpleCV import Image

img = Image('starry_night.png')

# Generate the histogram with 256 bins, one for each color
histogram = img.histogram(256)

# Show how many elements are in the list
len(histogram)
```

This will report 256 bins. As much fun as it is to look at lists of numbers, it is usually more intuitive to plot these in a chart. This is done with the plot() function.

```
from SimpleCV import Image

img = Image('starry_night.png')

# Generate the histogram with 256 bins, one for each color
histogram = img.histogram(256)

# Graphically display the histogram
plot(histogram)
```

The resulting figure should look like Figure 6-6.

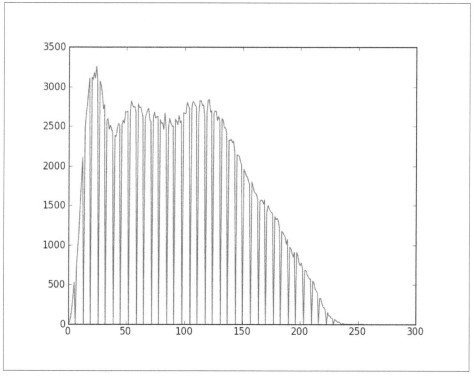

Figure 6-6. Histogram of The Starry Night

This histogram in Figure 6-6 indicates that a lot of pixels have very low values, representing dark shades. Given the original picture, this should not be surprising. A brighter picture would have a graph that was shifted further to the right. Rather than looking at the overall histogram, it is sometimes more useful to split the image into its individual color channels to look at the balance of color. This is demonstrated in the next example.

```
from SimpleCV import Image

img = Image('starry_night.png')

# Extract the three color channels
(red, green, blue) = img.splitChannels(False)  ❶

# The individual histograms
red_histogram = red.histogram(255)  ❷
green_histogram = green.histogram(255)
blue_histogram = blue.histogram(255)

# Plot the histograms
plot(red_histogram)  ❸
plot(green_histogram)
plot(blue_histogram)
```

❶ The splitChannels() function creates three images. The three images contain the red components, the green components, and the blue components, respectively. By default, this actually creates three grayscale images, showing the intensity of each individual color. By passing the parameter False, it keeps the original color, which is more intuitively appealing.

❷ After the individual color channels are split apart, then generate the histogram as was done in the grayscale example. Three channels means three histograms. The three histograms are displayed in Figure 6-7.

❸ Plot the histograms. Note that each plot command blocks the display of the next plot until the original histogram window is closed. In other words, the code will first show the red histogram. The green histogram will not be displayed until the red histogram window is closed. Then the blue histogram will not be displayed until the green window is closed.

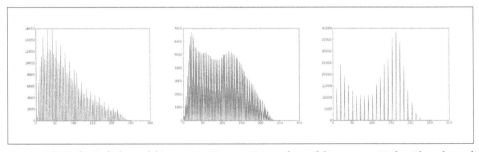

Figure 6-7. Left: Red channel histogram; Center: Green channel histogram; Right: Blue channel histogram

---

Histograms are very important when calibrating a camera. They are used to make sure that the exposure level is correct. Consider the example image in Figure 6-8. The picture on the left is a good photo of the painting. The center image is an overexposed version of the same photo. This is evident from the washed out white areas around the stars that used to be yellow. The histogram demonstrated this problem. Notice that it has a large spike at the far right of the graph. This indicates a lot of white. A well balanced histogram tends to look like a hump, without large spikes at either the dark or light end of the spectrum, similar to what was shown in Figure 6-6.

Figure 6-8. Upper Left: The regular picture; Center: Over-exposed picture; Right: Histogram for over-exposed picture

The above example works well for the white balance of an image. True imaging afi-cionados should perform a similar exercise on the three color channels as well to ensure that each individual color is also in balance.

Using Hue Peaks

After looking at the distribution of different colors in an image, the next logical question is to identify the dominant color in an image. This is known as finding the hue peaks and it is done using the huePeaks() function to find the dominant color(s).

Although an image could be first converted into the HSV format and then a histogram computed to get the hue information, the SimpleCV framework has a shortcut to do this on any image format. It is the hueHistogram() function. It works just like the standard histogram() function.

```
from SimpleCV import Image

img = Image('monalisa.png')

# Get the histogram
histogram = img.hueHistogram()

plot(histogram)

# Get the hue peaks
peaks = img.huePeaks()
```

```
# Prints: [(12.927374301675977, 0.11747342828238252)]
print peaks
```

The output of the huePeaks() function is an array of tuples. If there is a single dominant peak, then there is only one element in the array. The first value of the tuple is the bin that occurs most frequently. The second value is the percent of pixels that match that color. For example, in the example above, bin 13 is the most common, and appears 12% of the time. This should appear approximately correct given the histogram of the Mona Lisa image in Figure 6-9.

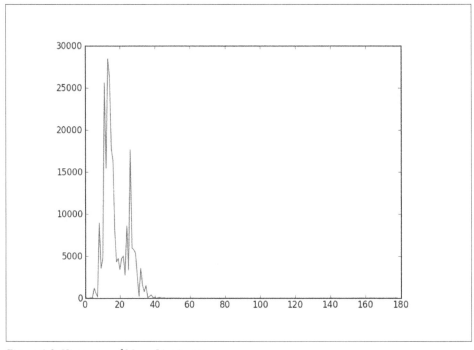

Figure 6-9. Histogram of Mona Lisa image

This data can be used to subtract out the less frequent hues. This trick is similar to the previous examples, which subtract values based on the color distance.

```
from SimpleCV import Image

img = Image('monalisa.png')

# Find the dominant hue
peaks = img.huePeaks()
peak_one = peaks[0][0]        ❶

# Get the hue distance to create a mask
hue = img.hueDistance(peak_one)      ❷
mask = hue.binarize().invert()       ❸
```

```
# Subtract out the dominant hue
lessBackground = img - mask  ❹

lessBackground.show()
```

❶ The function huePeaks() returns an array of tuples. The first [0] returns the first (and only) element of the array. The second [0] returns the first value of the tuple, which corresponds to the most frequently occurring hue.

❷ The hueDistance() function is similar to the colorDistance() function introduced in Chapter 4. (See earlier comments about the benefits of hue in HSV versus color in RGB.) It returns an image representing the distance of each pixel from the peak. Smaller values, which appear black, are close to the dominant hue. Larger values, which appear white, are farther from the dominant hue.

❸ Binarize the distance image, eliminating the shades of grey. This means that the mask can either subtract out the entire pixel or does not touch it.

❹ Subtract the mask from the original image. The parts of the mask that are white, erase corresponding pixels. The parts that are black do not have an effect. See Figure 6-10 for details.

Figure 6-10. Left: Mona Lisa image; Center: Mask removing the most common hue; Right: Part of the background removed

 There's still a moderate amount of noise left in the background. Tricks like the morphology functions covered in Chapter 4 can help clean up the mask.

Binary Masking

In the previous examples we show how to make a mask by using image math. The SimpleCV framework includes a shortcut method for standard masking operations as well. It is a binary mask function that masks out specific colors. The following example shows how to extract the face from the Mona Lisa. Results are shown in Figure 6-11.

```
from SimpleCV import Image

img = Image("monalisa.png")

mask = img.createBinaryMask(color1=(130,125,100),color2=Color.BLACK)  ❶

mask = mask.morphClose()  ❷

result = img - mask.invert()  ❸

result.show()
```

❶ Create a binary mask that masks out any colors in the range between `color1` and `color2`.

❷ Use a `morphClose()` to clean up some noise in the image.

❸ Apply the mask to the original image (result shown in Figure 6-11).

Examples

The examples for this chapter include two tricks for applying basic arithmetic to images. In the first example, multiple images are added together to create a motion blur effect. The second example shows how to use a green screen to put a foreground object into a different background scene.

Creating a Motion Blur Effect

One of the classic tricks in artistic photography is to use a long exposure. By leaving the camera shutter open, it creates a blur effect as objects move through the field of view. Although web cameras do not have shutters to directly replicate this effect, it can be simulated by adding together a series of images, effectively creating a motion blur.

```
from SimpleCV import Camera, Display

frameWeight = .2  ❶

cam = Camera()

lastImage = cam.getImage()

display = Display( (cam.getProperty('width'), cam.getProperty('height')) )
```

Figure 6-11. Result of the binary mask

```
while not display.isDone():
    img = cam.getImage()
    img = (img * frameWeight) + (lastImage * (1 - frameWeight))  ❷

    img.save(display)
    lastImage = img  ❸
```

❶ This controls the amount of blur. It means that 20% of the image will be the most recently captured image, with 80% coming from the previous frames.

❷ To implement the weighting, the first image is multiplied by 0.2 and the previous frame is multiplied by `1 - 0.2 = 0.8`. It is important that the sum of these weights equals 1. If less than one, the screen will grow very dark. If greater than 1, the screen will eventually become white.

❸ Finally, keep track of the image so that it can be used on the next iteration of the loop.

An example of the output is demonstrated in Figure 6-12.

Figure 6-12. Blur example

The result is not quite as smooth as a long exposure, but it has a similar effect. Generally, the quality of this trick increases as a larger number of images are captured in a fixed period of time.

Chroma Key (Green Screen)

The final example for this chapter is simulating a green screen. This is a classic trick in television or movie productions. The weather reporter on the evening news typically stands in front of a green screen, and then weather maps are painted onto the green background by a computer. It's also a classic tool used in movies to add an actor to a background or an environment without the actor actually being there. Technically, there is nothing magical about the color green in a green screen. Other colors can be used instead. However, because the computer is performing a substitution based on the particular color, it is important to make sure that the reporter or actor is not also wearing that color. Otherwise, the computer will paint the background onto the actor as well.

The following example lets anyone with a webcam play weather man, and look like they're located in front of a weather map such as the one shown in Figure 6-13. Of course, this example works best with an evenly lit green screen. However, any solid colored background should work, though it may create some problems. (As Figure 6-14 demonstrates, sometimes standing in front of a white wall creates problems with shiny balding heads.) The greater the color difference between the background color and the person/object in the foreground, the better this example works.

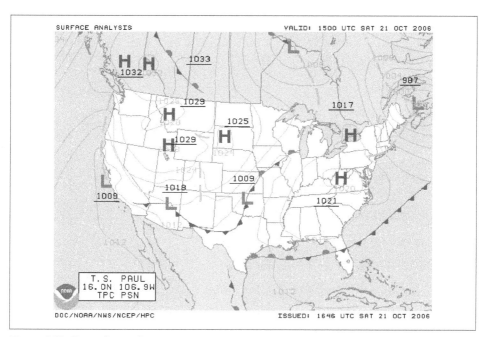

Figure 6-13. Example weather map

Figure 6-14. Result of green screen

```
from SimpleCV import Camera, Color, Display, Image

cam = Camera()
background = Image('weather.png')  ❶

disp = Display()

while not disp.isDone():
    img = cam.getImage()
    img = img.flipHorizontal()  ❷

    bgcolor = img.getPixel(10, 10)  ❸
    dist = img.colorDistance(bgcolor)  ❹
    mask = dist.binarize(50)  ❺

    foreground = img - mask  ❻

    background = background - mask.invert()  ❼

    combined = background + foreground  ❽

    combined.save(disp)
```

❶ This loads the background image of a weather map.

❷ Grab an image with the webcam. Mirror the image so that motions made in front of the webcam more intuitively match what is displayed on the screen.

❸ Rather than hardcode the color for the background, assume that the pixel at the coordinates (10, 10) is the background color.

❹ Find the color distance between each pixel and the background color. This is used to distinguish between foreground and background pixels.

❺ Because most pixels on the screen will have some similarity to the background color, binarize the image. This ensures that the foreground components are pure black and the background components are pure white.

❻ By subtracting the mask from the foreground image, all of the background pixels are zeroed out and the foreground pixels are left untouched.

❼ Subtract the inverse of the mask from the background; it will create a hole in the image where the foreground image can be inserted.

❽ Finally, put the two images together.

## CHAPTER 7

Drawing on Images

Vision systems usually need to provide some form of feedback to its users. Although this could be in the form of messages printed to a log, a spreadsheet, or other data output, users are most comfortable with graphical output, in which key information is drawn directly on the image. This feedback is often more user-friendly because it is noticeable and can give the user more context about the message. When the program claims to have found features on an image, which ones did it find? Was it picking up noise? Is it finding the right objects? Even if the program will ultimately run without any user interaction, this type of feedback during development is vital. If, on the other hand, the system is designed to have users interacting with it, then drawing on images can be an important means for improving the user interface. For example, if the system measures several different objects, rather than printing a list of measurements to a console, it would be easier for the operator if the measurements were printed directly on the screen next to each object. This spares the operator from having to guess which measurements correspond to the different objects on the screen or trying to estimate which object is the correct one based on their coordinates.

The SimpleCV framework has a variety of methods for drawing on and marking up images. Some of these are standard tools, found in most basic image manipulation programs. These are functions like drawing boxes, circles, or text on the screen. The SimpleCV framework also includes features more commonly found in intermediate or higher end applications, such as manipulating layers. In general, this chapter covers:

- A review of the `Display` object and how images interact with it
- An introduction to layers and the default Drawing Layer
- Drawing lines and circles
- Manipulating text and its various characteristics such as color, font, text size, and so on.

The Display

Rather than recklessly diving right into drawing, it would be helpful to first understand the canvas. In Chapter 2, the `Display` object was introduced. This represents the window in which the image is displayed. The SimpleCV framework currently only supports a single display window at a time and only one image can be displayed in that window. In most cases, the display is automatically created based on the size of the image to be displayed. However, if the display is manually initialized, the image will be automatically scaled or padded to fit into the display.

 To work around the single display limitation, two images can be pasted side-by-side into a single larger image. The `sideBySide()` function does this automatically. For example, `img1.sideBySide(img2)` will place the two images side by side. Then these two images can be drawn to the single window, helping to work around the single window limitation.

```
from SimpleCV import Display, Camera, Image

display = Display(resolution = (800, 400))  ❶

cam = Camera(0, {'width': 320, 'height': 240})  ❷

img = cam.getImage()

img.save(display)  ❸

# Should print: (320, 240)
print img.size()
```

❶ Initialize the display. Notice that the display's resolution is intentionally set to a very strange aspect ratio. This is to demonstrate how the image then fits into the resulting window.

❷ Initialize the camera. The camera is intentionally initialized with smaller dimensions and a different aspect ratio than the display.

❸ As mentioned in Chapter 1, "saving" an image to the display shows it in the window.

Notice the result in this case. The window remains 800×400. The image is scaled up so that the height now matches the 400 pixels of the window. Then padding is added to the left and right sides. The effect is similar to the `adaptiveScale()` function. The original image size is not altered. You can see this effect in Figure 7-1. It remains 320×240 as is shown in the print statement, but it is scaled for display.

Figure 7-1. Left: The image as captured by the camera; Right: The image was scaled up so that it vertically filled the display, and then padding is added to the right and left to horizontally fill the display

Images can also be divided into layers. Layers act like multiple images that sit on top of each other. The order of the layers is important. Items on the top layer cover items in the same area on the layer beneath it. Otherwise, if there is nothing covering them, the items from the lower layers will show through. Although all processing could be done on a single layer of an image, multiple layers can simplify processing. For example, the original image can sit on the bottom layer, and then lines drawn around the edges of objects can appear on the next layer up. Then, text describing the object can sit on the top layer. This preserves the original image while ensuring that the drawings and markup appear to the end user.

Working with Layers

With the preliminaries aside, it is time to start drawing. Layers are implemented in the `DrawingLayer` class. For those who have previous experience working with PyGame, a `DrawingLayer` is a wrapper around PyGame's `Surface` class. This class has features for drawing text, managing fonts, drawing shapes, and generally marking up an image. Remember that one key advantage is that this all occurs on a layer above the main image, leaving the original image intact. This enables convenient markup while preserving the image for analysis.

 When saving an image with layers, the saved image is flattened—all of the data is merged together so that it appears as a single layer. The `Image` object itself remains separated into layers.

One of the easiest examples of using a layer is to draw one image on top of another. The following example demonstrates how to insert yourself into the classic *American Gothic* painting (by Grant Wood), as demonstrated in Figure 7-2.

Figure 7-2. American Gothic by Grant Wood

```
from SimpleCV import Image

head = Image('head.png')

amgothic = Image('amgothic.png')

amgothic.dl().blit(head, (175, 110))   ❶

amgothic.show()
```

❶ The dl() function is just a shortcut for the getDrawingLayer() function. Because the layer did not already exist, dl() created the layer so that it could hold the face. Then blit() function—which is short for BLock Image Transfer—copied the provided image onto the background. The first parameter is the image to add, the second parameter is the coordinate at which to add the image.

The resulting program adds a third person into the image, as demonstrated in Figure 7-3.

Figure 7-3. Three's a crowd

 The blit() function can be used without layers, too. For example, new Image = amgoth.blit(head) creates a new flat image (without layers) that appears exactly the same. However, in this case, the face is copied right onto the main image and any information about the original pixels that are covered in that spot are lost.

A lot of stuff is happening under the hood in the previous example. To look at this in more detail, consider the following example, which works with the underlying layers:

```
from SimpleCV import Image, DrawingLayer

amgothic = Image('amgothic.png')

size = amgothic.size()

# Prints the image size: (468, 562)
print size

# Prints something like: [<SimpleCV.DrawingLayer object size (468, 562)>]
print amgothic.layers()  ❶
```

```
layer1 = DrawingLayer(size)  ❷

amgothic.addDrawingLayer(layer1)   ❸

# Prints information for two DrawingLayer objects
print amgothic.layers()
```

The above code essentially manually does everything that was done earlier with back
ground.dl(). Obviously this is more complex, but it shows in more detail how to work
with layers:

❶ The layers() property represents the list of all of the layers on the image.

❷ This creates a new drawing layer. By passing DrawingLayer() a tuple with the width
and height of the original image, it creates a new layer that is the same size. At this
point, the layer is not attached to the image.

❸ The addDrawingLayer() function adds the layer to the image, and appends it as the
top layer. To add a layer in a different order, use the insertDrawingLayer() function
instead.

The above process—creating a drawing layer and then adding it to an image—can be
repeated over and over again. The layer added in the example above does not do anything yet. The next example shows how to get access to the layers so that they can be
manipulated.

```
# This code is a continuation of the previous block of example code

# Outputs: 2
print len(amgothic.layers())

drawing = amgothic.getDrawingLayer()  ❶

drawing = amgothic.getDrawingLayer(1)  ❷
```

❶ Using getDrawingLayer() without an argument causes the function to return the
topmost drawing layer.

❷ In this case, since 1 was passed in as an argument, the function returns the drawing
layer that has 1 as its index number.

In the previous examples, a drawing layer is first created, and then that drawing layer
is added to an image. The layer is not actually fixed to the image. Instead, a layer from
one image can actually be applied to another image. The following example builds off
the first example in this chapter, where a face was placed on an image. This re-extracts
the face from a layer, and then copies that whole layer to a new image.

```
from SimpleCV import Image, DrawingLayer

head = Image('head.png')

amgothic = Image('amgothic.png')
```

```
scream = Image('scream.png')

amgothic.dl().blit(head, (175, 110))  ❶

layer = amgothic.getDrawingLayer()  ❷

scream.addDrawingLayer(layer)  ❸

scream.show()
```

❶ Up to this point, the example is similar to what we have seen before. This line adds the third head onto the American Gothic image.

❷ We then extract the layer back from the American Gothic image using the `getDra wingLayer()` function. In this case, there is just one layer, so no index is required when retrieving the layer.

❸ Next, copy that layer to the image of The Scream. This will add a floating head above the screaming person in the original image. Note that even though the layer from the American Gothic image is a different size than The Scream image, the layer can still be copied.

The resulting image will look like Figure 7-4.

As demonstrated above, when copying a layer between images, the same layer is actually shown on both images. In other words, when a layer is modified, the resulting change appears on both images.

```
# This is a continuation of the previous block of example code

print amgothic._mLayers  ❶
print scream._mLayers

layer.blit(head, (75, 220))  ❷

amgothic.show()  ❸
scream.show()
```

❶ These two print statements should print out identical information, showing that it's the same object.

❷ By passing the coordinates (75, 220) into the `blit` function, you are adding a second copy of the head image to the layer.

❸ Even though the layer was changed in one spot, the result propagates to both images.

Notice that now the change appears on both images, as demonstrated in Figure 7-5.

Figure 7-4. A face that would make anyone want to scream

Drawing

The SimpleCV framework includes tools to draw several basic shapes such as lines, bezier curves, circles, ellipses, squares, and polygons. To demonstrate the true power of the drawing engine, Figure 7-6 is a rendering of a lollipop (there is a reason we did not go to art school):

```
from SimpleCV import Image, Color

img = Image((300,300))  ❶

img.dl().circle((150, 75), 50, Color.RED, filled = True)  ❷

img.dl().line((150, 125), (150, 275), Color.WHITE, width = 5)  ❸

img.show()
```

❶ This creates a blank 300×300 image.

❷ Fetches the drawing layer and draws a filled red circle on it.

❸ Fetches the drawing layer and draws a white line on it that is 5 pixels wide.

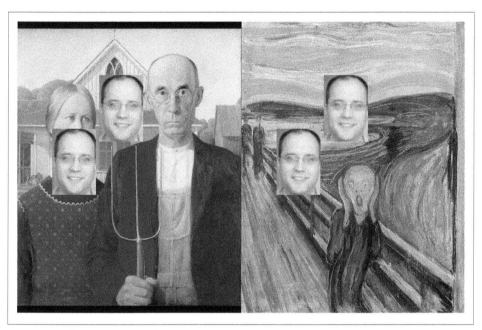

Figure 7-5. The picture was added to the layer, making it appear on both images

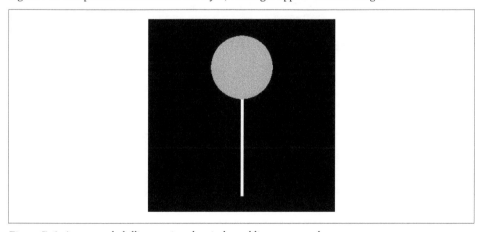

Figure 7-6. An example lollipop using the circle and line commands

Most of the time, rather than drawing on a blank image, we want to mark up existing data. Here, we show how to mark up the camera feed to make it easier to find and calibrate the center by adding markup similar to a scope (see Figure 7-7):

```
from SimpleCV import Camera, Color, Display

cam = Camera()
size = cam.getImage().size()
```

```
disp = Display(size)

center = (size[0] /2, size[1] / 2)


while disp.isNotDone():
    img = cam.getImage()

    # Draws the inside circle
    img.dl().circle(center, 50, Color.BLACK, width = 3)   ❶

    # Draws the outside circle
    img.dl().circle(center, 200, Color.BLACK, width = 6)  ❷

    # Draw the radiating lines
    img.dl().line((center[0], center[1] - 50), (center[0], 0),
        Color.BLACK, width = 2)
    img.dl().line((center[0], center[1] + 50), (center[0], size[1]),
        Color.BLACK, width = 2)
    img.dl().line((center[0] - 50, center[1]), (0, center[1]),
        Color.BLACK, width = 2)
    img.dl().line((center[0] + 50, center[1]), (size[0], center[1]),
        Color.BLACK, width = 2)

    img.save(disp)
```

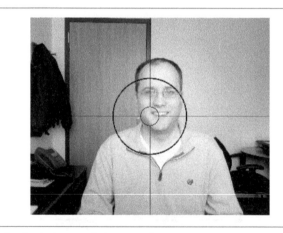

Figure 7-7. Example of painting crosshairs on an image

We can also manage layers independently of images. Because the scope marks are the same in each frame, we can draw them once and apply the layer to subsequent images. This reduces the amount of processing that must be done on each frame.

```
from SimpleCV import Camera, Color, Display, DrawingLayer

cam = Camera()

size = cam.getImage().size()
```

```
disp = Display(size)

center = (size[0] /2, size[1] / 2)

# Create a new layer and draw on it
scopelayer = DrawingLayer(size)

# This part works just like the previous example
scopelayer.circle(center, 50, Color.BLACK, width = 3)
scopelayer.circle(center, 200, Color.BLACK, width = 6)
scopelayer.line((center[0], center[1] - 50), (center[0], 0),
    Color.BLACK, width = 2)
scopelayer.line((center[0], center[1] + 50), (center[0], size[1]),
    Color.BLACK, width = 2)
scopelayer.line((center[0] - 50, center[1]), (0, center[1]),
    Color.BLACK, width = 2)
scopelayer.line((center[0] + 50, center[1]), (size[0], center[1]),
    Color.BLACK, width = 2)


while disp.isNotDone():
    img = cam.getImage()

    # Rather than a lot of drawing code, now we
    # can just add the layer to the image
    img.addDrawingLayer(scopelayer)

    img.save(disp)
```

When using markup on images, it's often a good idea to use it to highlight regions of
interest, as in this example which uses the parking photo first demonstrated in Chapter 4. To demonstrate to the application user the part of the image that will be cropped,
we can draw a box around the relevant region:

```
from SimpleCV import Image, Color, DrawingLayer

car = Image('parking-car.png')

boxLayer = DrawingLayer((car.width, car.height))  ❶

boxLayer.rectangle((400, 100), (400, 400), color=Color.RED)  ❷

car.addDrawingLayer(boxLayer)  ❸

car.show()
```

❶ First, construct a new drawing layer to draw the box.

❷ Next, draw a rectangle on the layer using the rectangle() function. The first tuple
is the (x, y) coordinates of the upper left corner of the rectangle. The second tuple
represents the height and width of the rectangle. It is also colored red to make it
stand out more.

❸ Now add the layer with the rectangle onto the original image.

This block of code produces output as demonstrated in Figure 7-8.

Figure 7-8. Bounding box drawn around the yellow car

This layer can then be used to compare the crop region with the parking image without a car. This will help to compare the regions of interest between the two versions of the photos.

```
# This is a continuation of the previous example

nocar = Image('parking-no-car.png')

nocar.addDrawingLayer(boxLayer)
```

This works just like the previous example, except that now it shows the region of interest on the similar image without the illegally parked car. The resulting photo should look like Figure 7-9.

For a slight variation on the above example, drawing circles on the image could help to identify the distance between objects. For example, using the same example image as above, assume that 100 pixels is about 3 feet. How far away is the Volvo on the left from the illegal parking spot? One way to visually estimate the distance is to draw a series of concentric circles radiating out from the handicap parking space, as shown in Figure 7-9.

Figure 7-9. Box showing where the car is in the other picture

```
from SimpleCV import Image, Color, DrawingLayer

car = Image('parking-car.png')

parkingSpot = (600, 300)  ❶

circleLayer = DrawingLayer((car.width, car.height))  ❷

circleLayer.circle(parkingSpot, 100, color=Color.RED)  ❸
circleLayer.circle(parkingSpot, 200, color=Color.RED)
circleLayer.circle(parkingSpot, 300, color=Color.RED)
circleLayer.circle(parkingSpot, 400, color=Color.RED)
circleLayer.circle(parkingSpot, 500, color=Color.RED)

car.addDrawingLayer(circleLayer)  ❹

car.show()
```

❶ Because this example draws a bunch of concentric circles, it is easier to simply define the center once rather than constantly retyping it. This point corresponds approximately to the middle of the handicap spot.

❷ This line of code should be familiar from the rectangle drawing example. Create a new drawing layer with the same dimensions as the underlying image.

❸ Draw the circle using the `circle()` function. The first parameter is the center of the circle, which was defined in step 1. The second parameter sets the radius of the circle. The third parameter sets the color. It defaults to black, so a red circle is specified to make it appear more obvious on the image.

❹ This line of code should now look familiar. It adds the new drawing layer to the image.

The resulting image should look like the image in Figure 7-10. Based on the image, the car is four to five circles away from the center of the handicap spot. Because the radius increased by 100 pixels per circle, that translates into 400 to 500 pixels. Under the rough assumption that 100 pixels equals three feet, then the Volvo is currently around 15 feet away from the center of the illegal parking space. It is probably safe to assume that it is legally parked.

Figure 7-10. Circles approximating distance from the car

 Chapter 8 demonstrates a more rigorous approach to measuring between objects on an image.

After all this drawing, it may be necessary to remove all the code and start over with a clean slate. To clear the image, use the clearLayers() function.

```
# This is a continuation of the previous example

car.clearLayers()

car.show()

print car.layers()
```

The car image is back to its original state before the circles were drawn. Visually, the circles no longer appear. When printing out a list of all the layers on the image, no layers appear. Note, however, that the original circleLayer object still exists. It can be placed back on the image with the addDrawingLayer() function.

This section did not cover all of the possible shapes, but it did present the standard approach. Several other frequently used options for drawing include:

Line: line(start=(x1, y1), end=(x2, y2))
    Draws a straight line between the two provided points.

Ellipses: ellipse(center=(x, y), dimensions = (width, height))
    Draws a "squished" circle.

Centered Rectangle: centeredRectangle(center=(x, y), dimensions=(x,y))
    Similar to rectangle(), except the center point is provided instead of the upper-left corner, in some cases saving some arithmetic.

Polygon: polygon(points = [(x1, y1), (x2, y2), (x3, y3) …])
    By providing a list of (x, y) points, this will draw lines between all connected points.

Bézier Curve: bezier(points = (p1, p1, p3, p4, …), steps=s)
    Draws a curve based on the specified control points and the number of steps.

Text and Fonts

Displaying text on the screen is fairly simple. In the previous example using circles to show distances, the example assumed that users knew that each circle was about three feet in radius. It would be better to mark those distances on the screen. Fortunately, drawing text on an image is just as easy as drawing shapes.

```
from SimpleCV import Image, Color, DrawingLayer

# This first part of the example is the same as before

car = Image('parking-car.png')

parkingSpot = (600, 300)

circleLayer = DrawingLayer((car.width, car.height))
```

```
circleLayer.circle(parkingSpot, 100, color=Color.RED)
circleLayer.circle(parkingSpot, 200, color=Color.RED)
circleLayer.circle(parkingSpot, 300, color=Color.RED)
circleLayer.circle(parkingSpot, 400, color=Color.RED)
circleLayer.circle(parkingSpot, 500, color=Color.RED)

car.addDrawingLayer(circleLayer)

# Begin new material for this example:

textLayer = DrawingLayer((car.width, car.height))  ❶

textLayer.text("3 ft", (500, 300), color=Color.RED)  ❷
textLayer.text("6 ft", (400, 300), color=Color.RED)
textLayer.text("9 ft", (300, 300), color=Color.RED)
textLayer.text("12 ft", (200, 300), color=Color.RED)
textLayer.text("15 ft", (100, 300), color=Color.RED)

car.addDrawingLayer(textLayer)

car.show()
```

Many of the components of this example should now be familiar based on previous examples. However, a couple of items are worth noting:

❶ This example adds the text to its own drawing layer. Technically, this could be done on the same layer as the circles, but this makes it easier to easily add/subtract the labels.

❷ To do the actual writing on the screen, use the text() function. The first parameter defines the actual text to be written to the screen. The second parameter is a tuple with the (x, y) coordinates of the upper left corner of the text. The final parameter defines the color as red to make it slightly easier to read.

The resulting image should look like Figure 7-11.

Figure 7-11. Distance circles with labels

Although the red colored font is slightly easier to read than a simple black font, the labels are still a bit difficult to read. A larger, easier-to-read font would help. Changing the font is relatively simple. The first step is to get a list of fonts that are available on the system. The `listFonts()` function will do the trick:

```
# This is a continuation of the previous example

textLayer().listFonts()
```

This prints a list of all the fonts installed on the system. Actual results will vary from system to system. The name of the font is just the part between the single quotation marks. For example, u'**arial**' indicates that the **arial** font is installed. The u prefix in front of some entries merely indicates that the string was encoded in unicode. Because **arial** is a pretty common font on many systems, it will be used in the following examples.

 The following examples may need to be adjusted slightly based on available fonts.

To change the font, simply insert code such as indicated below before calling the `text()` function:

```
# Code you could add to the previous example
```

```
textLayer.selectFont('arial')    ❶
textLayer.setFontSize(24)    ❷
```

❶ Select the font based on the name. This name is taken from the `listFonts()` function previously demonstrated.

❷ The font size is changed with the `setFontSize()` function.

If used with the previous example, the output will look like the example in Figure 7-12.

Figure 7-12. Circles with larger, easier-to-read labels

Several other font configuration commands are also available:

`setFontBold()`
    Make the font bold

`setFontItalic()`
    Make the font italic

`setFontUnderline()`
    Underline the text

One final way to make it easier to see the drawn material is to control the layer's transparency. By making it more opaque, it will mask the underlying material, making the drawn shapes and text stand out.

```
from SimpleCV import Image, Color, DrawingLayer

car = Image('parking-car.png')
```

```
parkingSpot = (600, 300)

circleLayer = DrawingLayer((car.width, car.height))

# This is the new part:
circleLayer.setLayerAlpha(175)

# The remaining sections is the same as before
circleLayer.circle(parkingSpot, 100, color=Color.RED)
circleLayer.circle(parkingSpot, 200, color=Color.RED)
circleLayer.circle(parkingSpot, 300, color=Color.RED)
circleLayer.circle(parkingSpot, 400, color=Color.RED)
circleLayer.circle(parkingSpot, 500, color=Color.RED)

car.addDrawingLayer(circleLayer)

textLayer = DrawingLayer((car.width, car.height))

textLayer.selectFont('arial')
textLayer.setFontSize(24)

textLayer.text("3 ft", (500, 300), color=Color.RED)
textLayer.text("6 ft", (400, 300), color=Color.RED)
textLayer.text("9 ft", (300, 300), color=Color.RED)
textLayer.text("12 ft", (200, 300), color=Color.RED)
textLayer.text("15 ft", (100, 300), color=Color.RED)

car.addDrawingLayer(textLayer)

car.show()
```

The one new line of code was using the setLayerAlpha function. This takes a single parameter of an alpha value between 0 and 255. An alpha of zero means that the background of the layer is transparent. If the alpha is 255, then the background is opaque. By setting it to a value of 175 in the example, the background is darkened but still visible, as is shown in Figure 7-13.

 Be careful when changing the alpha on multiple layers. If each layer progressively makes the background more opaque, they will eventually completely black out the background.

Examples

The two examples in this chapter demonstrate how to provide user feedback on the screen. The first example draws stop and go shapes on the screen in response to the amount of light captured on the camera. The second example expands on the crosshair code snippets above, integrating mouse events. Finally, the third example shows how to simulate a zoom effect in a window, controlled with the mouse wheel.

Figure 7-13. Partially transparent layer on top of the image

Making a Custom Display Object

This example is for a basic Walk or Don't Walk type scenario, as shown in Figure 7-14 and Figure 7-15. It detects hypothetical vehicles approaching based on whether the light is present. If it detects light, it will show a message on the screen saying STOP.

> This example code is intended to demonstrate layers and drawing. It is not intended to be an actual public safety application.

```
from SimpleCV import Camera, Color, Display, DrawingLayer, np

cam = Camera()

img = cam.getImage()

display = Display()

width = img.width
height = img.height

screensize = width * height

# Used for automatically breaking up image
divisor = 5
```

```
# Color value to detect blob is a light
threshold = 150

# Create the layer to display a stop sign
def stoplayer():
    newlayer = DrawingLayer(img.size())  ❶

    # The corner points for the stop sign's hexagon
    points = [(2 * width / divisor, height / divisor),
              (3 * width / divisor, height / divisor),
              (4 * width / divisor, 2 * height / divisor),
              (4 * width / divisor, 3 * height / divisor),
              (3 * width / divisor, 4 * height / divisor),
              (2 * width / divisor, 4 * height / divisor),
              (1 * width / divisor, 3 * height / divisor),
              (1 * width / divisor, 2 * height / divisor)
              ]

    newlayer.polygon(points, filled=True, color=Color.RED)  ❷

    newlayer.setLayerAlpha(75)  ❸

    newlayer.text("STOP", (width / 2, height / 2), color=Color.WHITE)  ❹

    return newlayer

# Create the layer to display a go sign
def golayer():
    newlayer = DrawingLayer(img.size())  ❺

    newlayer.circle((width / 2, height / 2), width / 4, filled=True,
                    color=Color.GREEN)

    newlayer.setLayerAlpha(75)

    newlayer.text("GO", (width / 2, height / 2), color=Color.WHITE)

    return newlayer


while display.isNotDone():
    img = cam.getImage()

    # The minimum blob is at least 10% of screen
    min_blob_size = 0.10 * screensize

    # The maximum blob is at most 80% of screen
    max_blob_size = 0.80 * screensize


    # Get the largest blob on the screen
    blobs = img.findBlobs(minsize=min_blob_size, maxsize=max_blob_size)

    # By default, show the go layer
    layer = golayer()
```

```
# If there is a light, then show the stop
if blobs:
    # Get the average color of the blob
    avgcolor = np.mean(blobs[-1].meanColor())

    # This is triggered by a bright light
    if avgcolor >= threshold:
        layer = stoplayer()

# Finally, add the drawing layer
img.addDrawingLayer(layer)    ❻

img.save(display)
```

❶ The stop sign will be a hexagon. The SimpleCV framework does not have a function specifically for drawing a hexagon; instead it needs a set of corner points that define the shape.

❷ Use the drawPolygon() function and the list of corner points to construct the stop sign.

❸ Set the layer's alpha in order to partially gray out the background. Although the background is still visible, this helps draw attention to the stop sign.

❹ Add text in the middle of the stop sign to say "Stop."

❺ The overall flow of this code is the same as in the previous steps, but it is slightly simpler because the sign is a circle instead of a hexagon.

❻ Finally, add the layer. Depending on whether the light was shined at the camera, this will be either the stop sign or the go sign.

Keep in mind that lighting conditions and other environmental factors will affect how this application works. Play around with the threshold values to adjust the assurance. Although a train/traffic detector is a somewhat silly application, it demonstrates the basic principles behind detecting an object on the screen and then changing the screen output to alert the user—a very common activity in vision systems.

Figure 7-14. Example display when it is safe to walk

Figure 7-15. Example display when it is not safe to walk

Moving Target

The next example is similar to the crosshairs example shown earlier in this chapter. However, unlike the earlier example that fixed the crosshairs in the middle of the screen, this example lets the user control where it is aiming by clicking the left mouse button.

```
from SimpleCV import Camera, Color, Display

cam = Camera()

size = cam.getImage().size()

disp = Display(size)

center = (size[0] /2, size[1] / 2)

while disp.isNotDone():
    img = cam.getImage()

    img = img.flipHorizontal()  ❶

    if disp.mouseLeft:
        center = (disp.mouseX, disp.mouseY)  ❷


    # The remainder of the example is similar to the
    # short version from earlier in the chapter

    # Inside circle
    img.dl().circle(center, 50, Color.BLACK, width = 3)
    # Outside circle
    img.dl().circle(center, 200, Color.BLACK, width = 6)

    # Radiating lines
    img.dl().line((center[0], center[1] - 50), (center[0], 0),
        Color.BLACK, width = 2)
    img.dl().line((center[0], center[1] + 50), (center[0], size[1]),
        Color.BLACK, width = 2)
    img.dl().line((center[0] - 50, center[1]), (0, center[1]),
        Color.BLACK, width = 2)
    img.dl().line((center[0] + 50, center[1]), (size[0], center[1]),
        Color.BLACK, width = 2)

    img.save(disp)
```

❶ The flipHorizontal() function makes the camera act more like a mirror. This step is not strictly necessary. However, because most users are likely using this while sitting in front of a monitor-mounted web cam, this gives the application a slightly more intuitive feel.

❷ Update the center point by looking for mouse clicks. The mouseLeft event is triggered when the user clicks the left mouse button on the screen. Then the center point is updated to the point where the mouse is clicked, based on the `mouseX` and `mouseY` coordinates.

 The `mouseLeft` button is triggered if the user presses the button. They do not need to release the button to trigger this. So clicking and holding the button while dragging the mouse around the screen will continuously update the crosshair location.

Image Zoom

The scroll wheel on a mouse is frequently used to zoom in or out on an object. Although most webcams do not have a zoom feature, this can be faked by scaling up (or down) an image, and then cropping to maintain the original image dimensions (see Figure 7-16). This example reviews how to interact with the display window, and it shows how to manage images when they are different sizes than the display window.

```
from SimpleCV import Camera, Display

cam = Camera()

disp = Display((cam.getProperty('width'), cam.getProperty('height')))

# How much to scale the image initially
scaleFactor = 2

while not disp.isDone():
    # Check for user input
    if disp.mouseWheelUp:          ❶
        scaleFactor *= 1.1
    if disp.mouseWheelDown:
        scaleFactor /= 1.1

    # Adjust the image size
    img = cam.getImage().scale(scaleFactor)   ❷

    # Fix the image so it still fits in the original display window
    if scaleFactor < 1:
        img = img.embiggen(disp.resolution)   ❸
    if scaleFactor > 1:
        img = img.crop(img.width / 2, img.height / 2,
                disp.resolution[0], disp.resolution[1], True)   ❹

    img.save(disp)
```

❶ Check if the mouse is scrolled up or down and scale the image accordingly. Each event increases or decreases the image size by 10%.

❷ This step does the actual scaling. Note that at this step, the image is no longer the same size as the display window.

❸ If the image is smaller than the display—as represented by a scale factor that is less than one—then it needs to be embiggened. Recall that `embiggen()` changes the canvas size of the image, but leaves the underlying image intact.

❹ If the image is larger than the display, crop it. This example assumes that it should zoom into the middle. That means that the crop region is defined based on the center of the image. It is cropped to the same dimensions as the display so that it will fit.

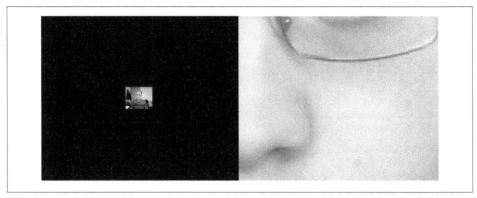

Figure 7-16. Left: Camera zoomed out; Right: Camera zoomed in

Basic Feature Detection

The human brain does a lot of pattern recognition to make sense of raw visual inputs. After the eye focuses on an object, the brain identifies the characteristics of the object —such as its shape, color, or texture—and then compares these to the characteristics of familiar objects to match and recognize the object. In computer vision, that process of deciding what to focus on is called feature detection. A feature in this sense can be formally defined as "one or more measurements of some quantifiable property of an object, computed so that it quantifies some significant characteristics of the object" (Kenneth R. Castleman, *Digital Image Processing*, Prentice Hall, 1996). An easier way to think of it, though, is that a feature is an "interesting" part of an image. What makes it interesting? Consider a photograph of a red ball on a gray sidewalk. The sidewalk itself probably isn't that interesting. The ball, however, is probably more interesting, because it is significantly different from the rest of the photograph. Similarly, when a computer analyzes the photograph, the gray pixels representing the sidewalk could be treated as background. The pixels that represent the ball probably convey more information, like how big the ball is or where on the sidewalk it lies.

A good vision system should not waste time—or processing power—analyzing the unimportant or uninteresting parts of an image, so feature detection helps determine which pixels to focus on. This chapter focuses on the most basic types of features: Blobs, Lines, Circles, and Corners. Features represent a new way of thinking about the image —rather than using the image as a whole, focus instead on just a few relevant pieces of an image.

Features also examine an image in a way that may be independent of a single image or other elements of the image. If the detection is robust, a feature is something that could be reliably detected across multiple images. For instance, with the red ball, the features of the ball do not really change based on the location of the ball in the image. The feature detection should work whether the ball is rolling or at rest. The shape and color of the ball should be the same in the lower left corner of the image as it would be in the upper right corner. Similarly, some changes in lighting conditions may change the color of the ball, but in many cases the hue will remain constant. This means that how we describe the feature can also determine the situations in which we can detect the feature.

Our detection criteria for the feature determines whether we can:

- Find the features in different locations of the picture (position invariant)
- Find the feature if it's large or small, near or far (scale invariant)
- Find the feature if it's rotated at different orientations (rotation invariant)

In this chapter, we examine the different things we can look for with feature detection, starting with the meat and potatoes of feature detection, the *Blob*.

Blobs

Blobs, also called objects or connected components, are regions of similar pixels in an image. This could be a group of brownish pixels together, which might represent food in a pet food detector. It could be a group of shiny metal looking pixels, which on a door detector would represent the door knob. A blob could be a group of matte white pixels, which on a medicine bottle detector could represent the cap. Blobs are valuable in machine vision because many things can be described as an area of a certain color or shade in contrast to a background.

 The term background in computer vision can mean any part of the image that is not the object of interest. It may not necessarily describe what is closer or more distant to the camera.

After a blob is identified, we can measure a lot of different things:

- A blob's area tells us how many pixels are in it.
- We can measure the dimensions such as width and height.
- We can find the center, based on the midpoint or the center of mass (also known as the centroid).
- We can count the number of blobs to find different objects.
- We can look at the color of blobs.
- We can look at its angle to see its rotation.
- We can find how close it is to a circle, square, or rectangle—or compare its shape to another blob.

Finding Blobs

At its most basic, `findBlobs()` can be used to find objects that are lightly colored in an image. If no parameters are specified, the function tries to automatically detect what is bright and what is dark. The following example looks for pennies, as shown in Figure 8-1:

```
from SimpleCV import Image

pennies = Image("pennies.png")

binPen = pennies.binarize()  ❶

blobs = binPen.findBlobs()  ❷

blobs.show(width=5)  ❸
```

❶ Blobs are most easily detected on a binarized image because that creates contrast between the feature in question and the background. This step is not strictly required on all images, but it makes it easier to detect the blobs.

❷ Since no arguments are being passed to the `findBlobs()` function, it returns a `FeatureSet` of the continuous light colored regions in the image. We'll talk about a `FeatureSet` in more depth in the next chapter, but the general idea is that it is a list of features about the blobs found. A `FeatureSet` also has a set of defined methods that are useful when handling features.

❸ Notice that the `show()` function is being called on blobs and not the `Image` object. The `show()` function is one of the methods defined with a `FeatureSet`. It draws each feature in the `FeatureSet` on top of the original image and then displays the results. By default, it draws the features in green and the function taks a `color` and `width` argument to customize the line. For instance, to draw the blobs in red, you could change the above code to `packs.show(Color.RED)`.

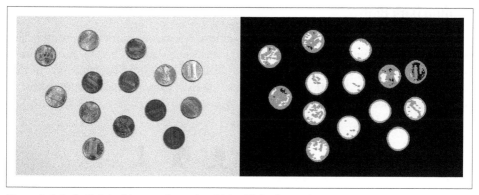

Figure 8-1. Left: Original image of pennies; Right: Blobs detected

The pennies are now green, as is shown in Figure 8-1. After the blob is found, several other functions provide basic information about the feature, such as its size, location, and orientation, as demonstrated in the next block of code:

```
from SimpleCV import Image

pennies = Image("pennies.png")
```

```
binPen = pennies.binarize()

blobs = binPen.findBlobs()

print "Areas: ", blobs.area()    ❶

print "Angles: ", blobs.angle()    ❷

print "Centers: ", blobs.coordinates()    ❸
```

❶ The area function returns an array of the area of each feature in pixels. By default, the blobs are sorted by size, so the areas should be ascending in size. The sizes will vary because sometimes it detects the full penny and other times it only detects a portion of the penny.

❷ The angle function returns an array of the angles, as measured in degrees, for each feature. The angle is the measure of rotation of the feature away from the x-axis, which is the 0 point. A positive number indicates a counter-clockwise rotation, and a negative number is a clockwise rotation.

❸ The coordinates function returns a two-dimensional array of the (x, y) coordinates for the center of each feature.

These are just a few of the available FeatureSet functions designed to return various attributes of the features. For information about these functions, see the FeatureSet section of this chapter.

Finding Dark Blobs

The findBlobs() function easily finds lightly colored blobs on a dark background. This is one reason why binarizing an image makes it easier to detect the object of interest. But what if the objects of interest are darkly colored on a light background? In that case, use the invert() function. For instance, the next example demonstrates how to find the chess pieces in Figure 8-2:

Figure 8-2. Black chess pieces

```
from SimpleCV import Image

img = Image("chessmen.png")

invImg = img.invert()    ❶

blobs = invImg.findBlobs()    ❷
```

```
blobs.show(width=2) ❸

img.addDrawingLayer(invImg.dl()) ❹

img.show()
```

❶ The `invert()` function turns the black chess pieces white and turns the white background to black.

❷ The `findBlobs()` function can then find the lightly colored blobs as it normally does.

❸ Show the blobs. Note, however, that this function will show the blobs on the inverted image, not the original image.

❹ To make the blobs appear on the original image, take the drawing layer from the inverted image (which is where the blob lines were drawn), and add that layer to the original image.

The result will look like Figure 8-3.

Figure 8-3. Top: The original image; Center: Blobs drawn on the inverted image; Bottom: Blobs on the original image

Finding Blobs of a Specific Color

The world does not consist solely of light and dark objects. In many cases, the actual color is more important than the brightness or darkness of the objects. The next example shows how to identify the blue candies in Figure 8-4.

To find the blobs that represent the blue candies, we use the color information returned from the `colorDistance()` function that we first introduced in Chapter 4 and later revisited in Chapter 5. Here's the example code:

```
from SimpleCV import Color, Image

img = Image("mandms.png")

blue_distance = img.colorDistance(Color.BLUE).invert() ❶

blobs = blue_distance.findBlobs() ❷
```

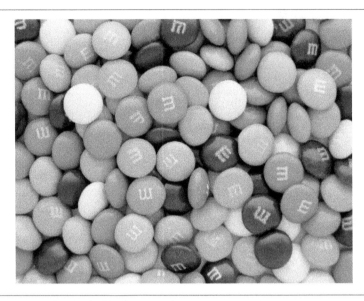

Figure 8-4. Everyone knows the blue ones are the tastiest

```
blobs.draw(color=Color.PUCE, width=3)  ❸

blue_distance.show()

img.addDrawingLayer(blue_distance.dl())  ❹

img.show()
```

❶ The `colorDistance()` function returns an image that shows how far away the colors in the original image are from the passed in `Color.BLUE` argument. To make this even more accurate, we could find the RGB triplet for the actual blue color on the candy, but this works well enough. Because any colors close to blue are black and colors far away from blue are white, we again use the `invert()` function to switch the target blue colors to white instead.

❷ We use the new image to find the blobs representing the blue candies. We can also fine-tune what the `findBlobs()` function discovers by passing in a threshold argument. The threshold can either be an integer or an RGB triplet. When a threshold value is passed in, the function changes any pixels that are darker than the threshold value to white and any pixels above the value to black.

❸ In the previous examples, we have used the `FeatureSet` `show()` method instead of these two lines (`blobs.show()`). That would also work here. We've broken this out into the two lines here just to show that they are the equivalent of using the other method. To outline the blue candies in a color not otherwise found in candy, they are drawn in puce, which is a reddish color.

❹ Similar to the previous example, the drawing ends up on the `blue_distance` image. Copy the drawing layer back to the original image.

The resulting matches for the blue candies will look like Figure 8-5.

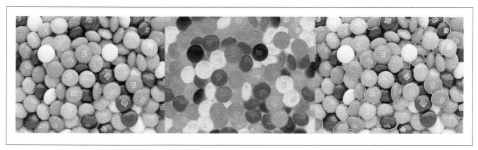

Figure 8-5. Left: the original image; Center: blobs based on the blue distance; Right: The blobs on the original image

Sometimes the lighting conditions can make color detection more difficult. To demonstrate the problem, Figure 8-6 is based on the original picture of the candies, but the left part of the image is darkened. The `hueDistance()` function is a better choice for this type of scenario. For instance, if the photo looked like Figure 8-6, where the right half is darkened, then `colorDistance()` wouldn't work very well on the right half. The right half of the image is intentionally very dark, but the following example shows how the colors can still be used to find blobs and provide a good example of why hue is more valuable than RGB color in cases where lighting may vary.

Figure 8-6. The candies with the right side darkened

To see how this is a problem, first consider using the previous code on this picture:

```
from SimpleCV import Color, Image

img = Image("mandms-dark.png")

blue_distance = img.colorDistance(Color.BLUE).invert()

blobs = blue_distance.findBlobs()

blobs.draw(color=Color.PUCE, width=3)

img.addDrawingLayer(blue_distance.dl())

img.show()
```

The results are shown in Figure 8-7. Notice that only the blue candies on the left are detected.

Figure 8-7. Finding blue candies with the dark right side

To resolve this problem use `hueDistance()` instead of `colorDistance()`. Because the hue is more robust to changes in light, the darkened right half of the image won't create a problem.

```
from SimpleCV import Color, Image

img = Image("mandms-dark.png")

blue_distance = img.hueDistance(Color.BLUE).invert() ❶

blobs = blue_distance.findBlobs()
```

```
blobs.draw(color=Color.PUCE, width=3)

img.addDrawingLayer(blue_distance.dl())

img.show()
```

❶ The one difference in this example is the use of the `hueDistance()` function. It works like the `colorDistance()` function, but notice that is produces better results, as indicated in Figure 8-8.

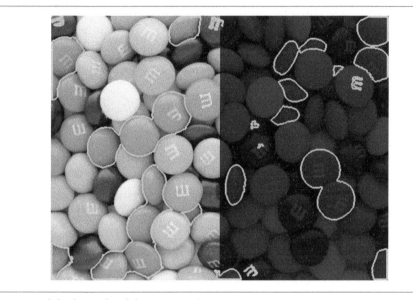

Figure 8-8. Blobs detected with hueDistance()

Lines and Circles

Lines

A line feature is a straight edge in an image that usually denotes the boundary of an object. It sounds fairly straightforward, but the calculations involved for identifying lines can be a bit complex. The reason is because an edge is really a list of (x, y) coordinates, and any two coordinates could possibly be connected by a straight line. For instance, Figure 8-9 shows four coordinates and two different examples of line segments that might connect those four points. It's hard to say which one is right—or if either of them are, since there are also other possible solutions. The way this problem is handled behind-the-scenes is by using the Hough transform technique. This technique effectively looks at all of the possible lines for the points and then figures out which

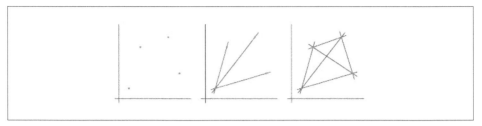

Figure 8-9. Left: Four coordinates; Center: One possible scenario for lines connecting the points; Right: An alternative scenario

lines show up the most often. The more frequent a line is, the more likely the line is an actual feature.

To find the line features in an image, use the `findLines()` function. The function itself utilizes the Hough transform and returns a `FeatureSet` of the lines found. The functions available with a `FeatureSet` are the same regardless of the type of feature involved. However, there are `FeatureSet` functions that may be useful when dealing with lines. These functions include:

`coordinates()`
> Returns the `(x, y)` coordinates of the starting point of the line(s).

`width()`
> Returns the width of the line, which in this context is the difference between the starting and ending `x` coordinates of the line.

`height()`
> Returns the height of the line, or the difference between the starting and ending `y` coordinates of the line.

`length()`
> Returns the length of the line in pixels.

The following code demonstrates how to find and then display the lines in an image. The example looks for lines on a block of wood.

```
from SimpleCV import Image

img = Image("block.png")

lines = img.findLines()     ❶

lines.draw(width=3)     ❷

img.show()
```

❶ The `findLines()` function returns a `FeatureSet` of the line features.

❷ This draws the lines in green on the image, with each line having a width of 3 pixels.

The lines found on the image are shown in Figure 8-10.

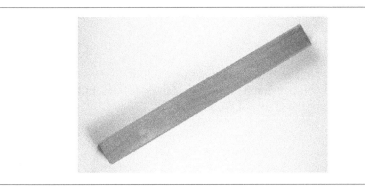

Figure 8-10. Example of basic line detection on a block of wood

Because this is just a simple block of wood in a well-lit environment, the `findLines()` function does a reasonable job finding the line features using the default values for its parameters. Many situations may require some tweaking to `findLines()` to get the desired results. For instance, notice that it found the long lines along the top and bottom of the block, but it did not find the lines along the side.

The `findLines()` function includes five different tuning parameters to help improve the quality of the results:

Threshold
    This sets how strong the edge should before it is recognized as a line.

Minlinelength
    Sets what the minimum length of recognized lines should be.

Maxlinegap
    Determines how much of a gap will be tolerated in a line.

Cannyth1
    This is a threshold parameter that is used with the edge detection step. It sets what the minimum "edge strength" should be.

Cannyth2
    This is a second parameter for the edge detection which sets the "edge persistence."

The threshold parameter for `findLines()` works in much the same way as the threshold parameter does for the `findBlobs()` function. If no threshold argument is provided, the default value it uses is set to 80. Lower threshold values result in more lines being found by the function; higher values result in fewer lines being found. Using the block of wood picture again, here's the code using a low threshold value:

```
from SimpleCV import Image

img = Image("block.png")

# Set a low threshold
lines = img.findLines(threshold=10)
```

```
lines.draw(width=3)

img.show()
```

Figure 8-11 shows what the resulting image would look like—with many more lines detected on the block. Notice that it found one of the side lines, but at the cost of several superfluous lines along the grains of wood.

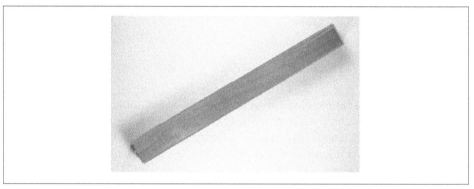

Figure 8-11. Line detection at a lower threshold

 If the threshold value for findLines() is set too high, then no lines will be found.

One way to get rid of small lines is to use the minlinelength parameter to weed out short lines. The length of a line is measured in pixels, and the default value find Lines() uses is 30 pixels long. In the example below, the minimum length is boosted, weeding out some lines.

```
from SimpleCV import Image

img = Image("block.png")

lines = img.findLines(threshold=10, minlinelength=50)

lines.draw(width=3)

img.show()
```

The result is shown in Figure 8-12. Notice that it eliminated a couple of the extra lines, but it came at a cost of eliminating the the side lines again.

Changing the line length doesn't solve the problem. The two ends of the image still are not found. In fact, it could create the opposite problem. Sometimes the algorithm may find very small lines and it needs to know whether those small line segments actually

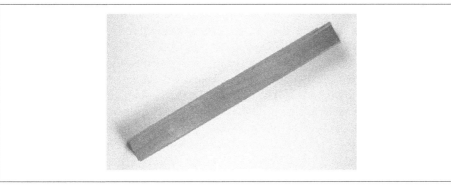

Figure 8-12. Line detection with an increased minimum length

represent one larger continuous line. The `findLines()` function can ignore small gaps in a line, and recognize it as the larger overall line. By default, the function combines two segments of a line if the gap between them is 10 pixels or less. Use the `maxline gap` parameter to fine tune how this works. The following example allows for a larger gap between lines, potentially allowing it to discover a few small lines that constitute the edge.

```
from SimpleCV import Image

img = Image("block.png")

lines = img.findLines(threshold=10, maxlinegap=20)

lines.draw(width=3)

img.show()
```

The result restores the right edge line again, but once again, it finds a lot of superfluous lines, as demonstrated in Figure 8-13.

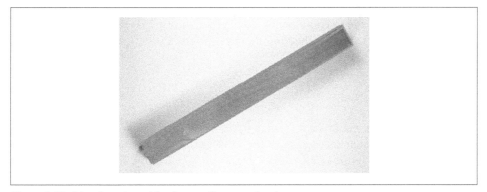

Figure 8-13. Line detection with a larger allowance for the gap

While setting the minimum line length decreased the number of lines found in the painting, adding in a longer gap then dramatically increased the number of lines. With the bigger gap, the line segments can be combined to meet the line length requirements and more lines are then recognized. The last two parameters, cannyth1 and cannyth2, are thresholds for the Canny edge detector. Roughly speaking, edges are detected by looking for changes in brightness. The first of these threshold parameters controls how much the brightness needs to change to detect an edge. The second parameter controls the threshold for linking together multiple edges. Both of these parameters act the same way as the previous three parameters: smaller values mean more lines will be detected, which could just be adding noise. Conversely, larger values will have less lines detected, but may mean that some valid lines aren't being returned. With all of these parameters, the trick is to work with the parameters until they are in the range that makes the most sense for the application.

Of course, sometimes it is easier to simply modify the image to reduce the noise rather than fine-tuning the parameters. The following example finds the desired lines on the block:

```
from SimpleCV import Image

img = Image('block.png')

dist = img.colorDistance((150, 90, 50))

bin = dist.binarize(70).morphClose()

lines = bin.findLines(threshold=10, minlinelength=15)

lines.draw(width=3)

# Move the lines drawn on the binary image back to the main image
img.addDrawingLayer(bin.dl())

img.show()
```

By binarizing the image, it eliminated a bunch of the noise that was causing the false-positive lines to appear where they should not. As a result, this draws lines around the block, as shown in Figure 8-14.

Circles

Circles are the next major feature that the SimpleCV framework can extract. The method to find circular features is called findCircle(), and it works the same way findLines() does. It returns a FeatureSet of the circular features it finds, and it also has parameters to help set its sensitivity. These parameters include:

Figure 8-14. Block with lines on all of the edges

Canny
> This is a threshold parameter for the Canny edge detector. The default value is 100. If this is set to a lower number, it will find a greater number of circles. Higher values instead result in fewer circles.

Thresh
> This is the equivalent of the `threshold` parameter for `findLines()`. It sets how strong an edge must be before a circle is recognized. The default value for this parameter is 350.

Distance
> Similar to the `maxlinegap` parameter for `findLines()`. It determines how close circles can be before they are treated as the same circle. If left undefined, the system tries to find the best value, based on the image being analyzed.

As with lines, there are `FeatureSet` functions that are more appropriate when dealing with circles, too. These functions include:

`radius()`
> As the name implies, this is the radius of the circle.

`diameter()`
> The diameter of the circle.

`perimeter()`
> This returns the perimeter of the feature, which in the case of a circle, is its circumference. It may seem strange that this isn't called circumference, but the term perimeter makes more sense when dealing with a non-circular features. Using perimeter here allows for a standardized naming convention.

To showcase how to use the `findCircle()` function, we'll take a look at an image of coffee mugs where one coffee mug also happens to have a ping-pong ball in it. Because there isn't any beer in the mugs, we'll assume that someone is very good at the game of beer pong—or perhaps is practicing for a later game? Either way, here's the example code:

```
from SimpleCV import Image

img = Image("pong.png")

circles = img.findCircle(canny=200,thresh=250,distance=15)  ❶

circles = circles.sortArea()  ❷

circles.draw(width=4)  ❸

circles[0].draw(color=Color.RED, width=4)  ❹

img_with_circles = img.applyLayers()  ❺

edges_in_image = img.edges(t2=200)  ❻

final = img.sideBySide(edges_in_image.sideBySide(img_with_circles)).scale(0.5)  ❼

final.show()
```

❶ Finds the circles in the image. We tested the values for the arguments we're using here to focus on the circles in which we're interested.

❷ The sortArea() function is used to sort the circles from the smallest one found to the largest. This lets us identify the circle that is the ping-pong ball, as it will be the smallest circle. It is possible to combine this step with the previous line, too—the result of this would be circles = img.findCircle(canny=200,thresh=250,distance=15).sortArea(). We only separated this into two steps in this example to make it easier to follow.

❸ This draws all of the circles detected in the green default color. The default line width is a little tough to see, so we're passing in an argument to increase the width of the line to 4 pixels (see Figure 8-15).

❹ This draws a circle in red around the smallest circle, which should be the ping-pong ball.

❺ The draw() function uses a drawing layer for the various circles. This line creates a new image that shows the original image with the drawn circles on top of it.

❻ In order to show the edges that the findCircle() function was working with, we use the edges() function to return an image of the edges found in the image. In order for the edges to be the same, we're passing in the same threshold value (200) to edges() as we did to findCircle(). For edges(), this threshold parameter is called t2, but it's the same thing as the canny parameter for findCircles().

❼ This combines the various images into a single image. The final result shows the original image, the image of the found edges, and then the original image with the circles drawn on top of it.

The next example combines finding both circle and line features by reading the line on a dial. These types of dials can be found in a variety of places, from large equipment to

Figure 8-15. Image showing the detected circles

lighting controls around the house. For our example, we'll use the dial in Figure 8-16 with four different settings. The code first searches for the dial in the images, and then searches for the line on each dial. Then it measures the angle of that line, and prints it on the image of the dial.

```
from SimpleCV import Image

# Load the images of four dials with different settings
img0 = Image("dial1.png")
img1 = Image("dial2.png")
img2 = Image("dial3.png")
img3 = Image("dial4.png")

# Store them in an array of images
images = (img0,img1,img2,img3)

# This stores the dial-only part of the images
dials = []

for img in images:
    circles = img.findCircle().sortArea()   ❶
    dial = circles[-1].crop()   ❷

    lines = dial.findLines(threshold=40,cannyth1=270,cannyth2=400)   ❸
    lines = lines.sortLength()   ❹
    lines[-1].draw(color=Color.RED)
```

Figure 8-16. An analog dial like those found in older thermostats

```
lineAngle = lines[-1].angle()  ❺

if (lines[-1].x < (dial.width / 2)):  ❻
    if (lines[-1].y < (dial.width / 2)):
        lineAngle = lineAngle - 180
    else:
        lineAngle = 180 + lineAngle

dial.drawText(str(lineAngle),10,10)
dial = dial.applyLayers()
dials.append(dial)

result = dials[0].sideBySide(dials[1].sideBySide(dials[2].sideBySide(dials[3])))  ❼
result.show()
```

❶ The first step is to find the dial on the image using the findCircle() function. The sortArea() function sorts the circles, and because the dial will be the largest circle, we know that it is circles[-1], the last one in the list.

❷ Calling the crop() function on a feature crops the image to just the area of the circle. This then stores the cropped image in the dial variable.

❸ Now call the findLines() function on the cropped image (stored in dial).

❹ The `sortLength()` function sorts the list of lines based on their length. Because the dial's indicator line is most likely the longest line in the image, this will make it easy to identify it in the image.

❺ The `angle()` function computes the angle of a line. This is the angle between the line and a horizontal axis connected at the leftmost point of the line.

❻ The angles computed in the previous step are correct when the line is on the right side of the dial, but are incorrect for our purposes when on the left side. This is because the angle is calculated from the leftmost point of the line and not the center of the dial. This block of code compensates for this by determining which quadrant the line is in on the left side, and then either adding or subtracting 180 degrees to show the angle as it if were being calculated from the center of the dial instead.

❼ After looping through all of the dials, create a single image with the results side by side, as shown in Figure 8-17.

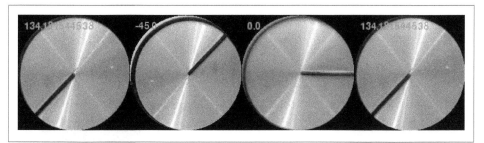

Figure 8-17. The results of the analog dial reader

Corners

Roughly speaking, corners are places in an image where two lines meet. Corners are interesting in terms of computer vision because corners, unlike edges, are relatively unique and effective for identifying parts of an image. For instance, when trying to analyze a square, a vertical line could represent either the left or right side of the square. Likewise, detecting a horizontal line can indicate either the top or the bottom. On the other hand, each corner is unique. For example, the upper left corner could not be mistaken for the lower right, and vice versa. This makes corners helpful when trying to uniquely identify certain parts of a feature.

The `findCorners()` function analyzes an image and returns the locations of all of the corners it can find. Note that a corner does not need to be a right angle at 90 degrees. Two intersecting lines at any angle can constitute a corner. As with `findLines()` and `findCircle()`, the `findCorners()` method returns a `FeatureSet` of all of the corner features it finds. While a corner's `FeatureSet` shares the same functions as any other `FeatureSet`, there are functions that wouldn't make much sense in the context of a corner. For example, trying to find the width, length, or area of a corner doesn't really make much sense. Technically, the functions used to find these things will still work, but what they'll return are default values and not real data about the corners.

Similar to the `findLines()` and `findCircle()` functions, `findCorners()` also has parameters to help fine-tune the corners that are found in an image. We'll walk through the available parameters using an image of a bracket as an example.

```
from SimpleCV import Image

img = Image('corners.png')

img.findCorners.show()
```

The little green circles in Figure 8-18 represent the detected corners. Notice that the example finds a lot of corners. By default, it looks for 50, which is obviously picking up a lot of false positives. Based on visual inspection, it appears that there are four main corners. To restrict the number of corners returned, we can use the `maxnum` parameter.

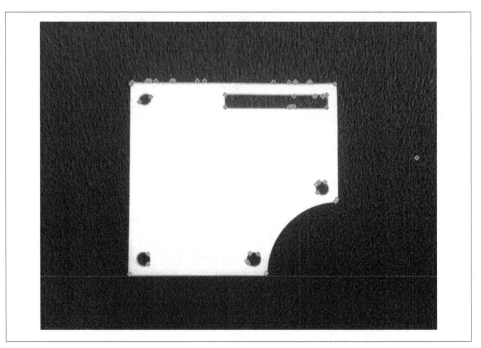

Figure 8-18. The corners found on a part

```
from SimpleCV import Image

img = Image('corners.png')

img.findCorners.(maxnum=9).show()
```

The findCorners() method sorts all of the corners prior to returning its results, so if it finds more than the maximum number of corners, it returns only the best ones (see Figure 8-19). Alternatively, the minquality parameter sets the minimum quality of a corner before it is shown. This approach filters out the noise without having to hard code a maximum number of corners for an object.

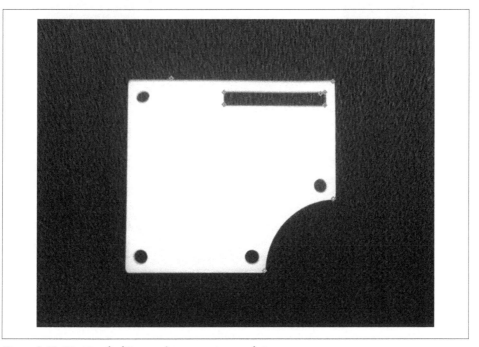

Figure 8-19. Limiting findCorners() to a maximum of nine corners

This is getting better, but the algorithm found two corners in the lower left and zero in the upper right. The two in the lower left are really part of the same corner, but the lighting and colors are confusing the algorithm. To prevent nearby corners from being counted as two separate corners, set the mindistance parameter, which sets the minimum number of pixels between two corners.

```
from SimpleCV import Image

img = Image('corners.png')

img.findCorners.(maxnum=9, mindistance=10).show()
```

The results of using a minimum distance are shown in Figure 8-20.

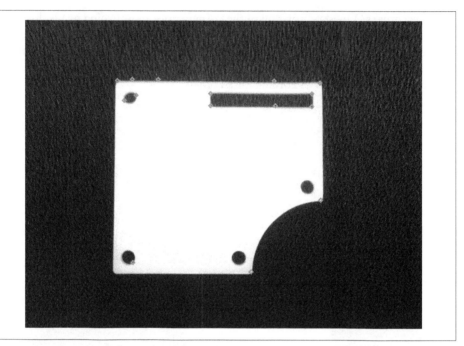

Figure 8-20. The corners when each corner is at least 10 pixels away from one another

Examples

In this example, we take a photo of some coins and calculate what their total value is. To do this, we find the blobs that represent each coin, and then compare them a table of their diameters to look up each coin's value. In the example, we presume we have a quarter among the coins to act as a reference object. The photo of the coins is shown in Figure 8-21.

```
from SimpleCV import Image, Blob
import numpy as np

img = Image("coins.png")

coins = img.invert().findBlobs(minsize = 500)  ❶

value = 0.0

# The value of the coins in order of their size
# http://www.usmint.gov/about_the_mint/?action=coin_specifications
coin_diameter_values = np.array([
    [ 19.05, 0.10],
    [ 21.21, 0.01],
    [ 17.91, 0.05],
    [ 24.26, 0.25]]);  ❷
```

Figure 8-21. A photo of some change

```
# Use a quarter to calibrate (in this example we must have one)
px2mm = coin_diameter_values[3,0] /  max([c.radius()*2 for c in coins])  ❸

for c in coins:
    diameter_in_mm = c.radius() * 2 * px2mm
    distance = np.abs(diameter_in_mm - coin_diameter_values[:,0])  ❹
    index = np.where(distance == np.min(distance))[0][0]  ❺
    value += coin_diameter_values[index, 1]  ❻

print "The total value of the coins is $", value
```

❶ We invert the image to make it easy to find the darker blobs that represent the coins, and eliminate small noisy objects by setting a minimum size.

❷ The `coin_diameter_values` array represents our knowledge about the relative sizes of the coins versus their values. The first entry in the array is for the smallest coin, a dime. The next largest coin is a penny, then a nickel, and finally a quarter. (This could easily be extended to include half dollars or dollar coins, based on their size.)

❸ We get a sense of scale by taking the largest diameter in our `FeatureSet` and assuming it's a quarter, similar to the Quarter for Scale example.

❹ This generates a list of distances that our blob radius is from each coin. Notice that it is slicing the diameter column of the value lookup table.

❺ This finds the index of the ideal coin to which the target is closest (minimizing the difference).

❻ Add the value from the diameter/value table to our total value.

When running this code using our example photo, the total value of the coins pictured should be $0.91. In this example, the basic detection was fairly straightforward, but we spent most of the time analyzing the data we gathered from the image. In the following chapter, we'll delve further into these techniques.

## CHAPTER 9

FeatureSet Manipulation

Up to this point in the book, features have generally been treated as singular objects. Yet in many cases, the goal is to work with a bundle of features, comparing them with each other, filtering the list of features, or generally extracting information from the set of features. In the SimpleCV framework, many features are bundles of numeric properties that can be manipulated using NumPy and SciPy, two Python libraries for managing (potentially very large and complex) tables of numbers. The kind of manipulations illustrated in this chapter provide an introduction to NumPy and SciPy, and for more details about working with these tools, see other books such as Eli Bresser's book, *SciPy and NumPy: An Overview for Developers*.

 NumPy has been briefly mentioned earlier in this book, but has not been formally introduced. NumPy is a Python library that provides support for large, multidimensional arrays and matrices. It also provides some numerical functions that can operate on those arrays and matrices. SciPy adds to this with a library of scientific functions for Python that span mathematics, science, and engineering. More information about NumPy is available from *http://numpy.scipy.org*, and for more on SciPy, visit *http://scipy.org*.

A FeatureSet is a list of features. From a programming perspective, this means that a FeatureSet is an extension of a Python list. Any Python tasks that work with a list also work with a FeatureSet. However, a FeatureSet is more than just a list. These functions typically fall into one of three camps: functions that perform a particular action on all the features in the set, functions that return properties of the individual features, or functions that order or group features together. These functions are designed to act on every feature within the set and returns properties as NumPy arrays, which enables further processing. This chapter reviews these FeatureSet functions, and provides illustrations of how they work.

Before diving into these features, the first step is to revisit a bit of Python's list functionality. With a Python list, individual elements of the list are accessed with index notation, such as myList[3] accessing the fourth element of the list. The same approach works with a FeatureSet. Using myFeatures[3] retrieves the fourth element of the set. Many of the examples in this book have used negative numbers as index values as well. When using a negative number, Python adds the length of the list to the negative value to get the appropriate index value, which makes it easier to pull elements from the end of the list instead of the beginning. For example, if a FeatureSet has five elements, myFeatures[-1] returns the fifth element. Like lists, FeatureSet slices, such as myFeatures[2:] returns all elements after the second element of the list. All of Python's list-specific functions, such as sort() or reverse(), work with FeatureSets as well.

Actions on Features

As mentioned before, the FeatureSet functions can be broken down into three categories. The first category is for functions that perform a particular action on all the features in a set. Some of these functions should look familiar by now and include:

draw()
>   Calls the draw() method on each feature in the set, rendering the feature to the image from which it was extracted

show()
>   This also calls the draw() method on each feature in the set, and then displays the image

crop()
>   This returns an image of each feature, cropped to the boundaries of that feature

image
>   This sets the image for each feature, which is useful when extracting features from images after running filters on them

> While they look the same, there is a difference between calling a function on a FeatureSet versus calling it on a feature. When calling a function on a FeatureSet, it calls the same method on every feature in the set. When calling a method on a Feature, it only impacts that single feature. In other words, given a FeatureSet named blobs, blobs.draw() draws all of the features, whereas blobs[0].draw() only draws the first feature in the set. Another way to think of this is that blobs.draw() is the same thing as writing [b.draw() for b in blobs].

The following example shows how to work with the image property of a FeatureSet. It is common to binarize an image before trying to detect features, but this creates a problem when displaying the features: the show or draw functions then display the features on the binarized image instead of the original image. (This idea was briefly addressed in Chapter 8.) To resolve this issue, set the FeatureSets image property to the original image; then all drawings will appear on the original image, as shown in Figure 9-1.

```
from SimpleCV import Image

img = Image("nuts-bolts.png")

nutsBolts = img.binarize().findBlobs()  ❶

nutsBolts.image = img  ❷

nutsBolts.show()  ❸
```

❶ The findBlobs() function returns a FeatureSet of the blobs it found on the binarized image of nuts and bolts. Because the function is called on the binarized image and not on the original image, any subsequent drawing will also be done on the binarized image.

❷ To correct the problem identified in the first step, set the image property. Now any drawing functions called will apply to the original image.

❸ This draws all of the blobs representing each nut and bolt back on to the original image and then displays it.

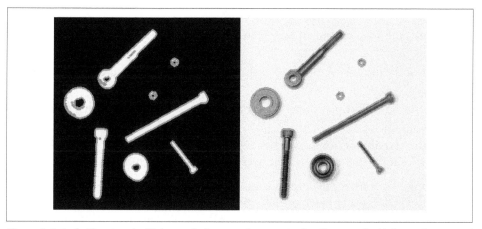

Figure 9-1. Left: Showing the blobs on the binarized image; Right: Showing the blobs on the original image

FeatureSet Properties

The second category of FeatureSet functions return a property of the features in the set. These functions return a NumPy array of the relevant feature. For example, the area() function returns a NumPy array of the areas of each feature detected. Because the results are returned as NumPy arrays, it is easy to use the NumPy or SciPy libraries for manipulation and processing.

The property methods include:

area()
    Returns the area (in pixels) of each feature

width()
    Returns the width of each feature in pixels

height()
    Returns the height of each feature in pixels

angle()
    Returns the angle for each feature. The angle is the measure of rotation of the feature away from the x-axis. Features with no angle always return 0.

length()
    Returns the longest dimension of each feature in pixels

coordinates()
    Returns a two-dimensional NumPy array of the (X, Y) coordinates of each feature (usually the midpoint).

x()
    Returns the X coordinate of each feature

y()
    Returns the Y coordinate of each feature

distanceFrom()
    Returns the distance in pixels of each feature from a given coordinate

meanColor()
    Returns the RGB triplet values for the average color of the area each feature covers

colorDistance()
    Returns the distance of the average color of each feature from a given color. If no color is supplied, it compares the average colors to the color black.

For an example, consider the previous example that detected blobs representing nuts and bolts. The following block of code differentiates between nuts and bolts. It does this by comparing the lengths of each object. Objects that are longer than the median length are determined to be bolts. Objects that are shorter than the median length are nuts. Nuts are drawn in red, bolts are drawn in green. It also prints out the lengths of the longest and shortest objects.

```
from SimpleCV import Color, Image
import numpy as np

img = Image('nuts-bolts.png')

blobs = img.binarize().findBlobs()
```

```
medSize = np.median(blobs.length())  ❶

blobs.image = img

for b in blobs:
    if (b.length() > medSize):  ❷
        b.draw(width=3, color=Color.GREEN)
    else:
        b.draw(width=3, color=Color.RED)

print 'The smallest length is ' + str(np.min(blobs.length()))  ❸
print 'The longest length is ' + str(np.max(blobs.length()))  ❹
```

❶ Use NumPy to compute the median length of all the items in the FeatureSet, both nuts and bolts.

❷ Assume that longer objects, based on being above the median length, are bolts, and therefore should be colored green. Otherwise, color the object red.

❸ Use NumPy's min() function to find the smallest length.

❹ Use NumPy's max() function to find the largest length.

The output should appear as shown in Figure 9-2.

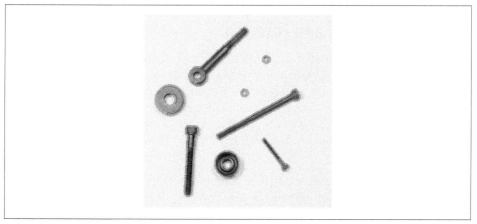

Figure 9-2. Bolts colored green, nuts colored red

As a slightly more advanced example, it is often important to measure the distance between objects. The following block of code examines the image of nuts and bolts to detect the pair of objects that are the closest and those that are the farthest apart.

```
from SimpleCV import Image
import scipy.spatial.distance as spsd  ❶
import numpy as np

img = Image("nuts-bolts.png")

blobs = img.binarize().findBlobs()
```

```
        distances = spsd.pdist(blobs.coordinates())  ❷

        print "Closest distance is ", np.min(distances)  ❸
        print "Longest  distance is ", np.max(distances)
```

❶ This example uses the `pdist()` function from the SciPy Spatial Distance library, and the `min()` and `max()` functions from the NumPy library.

❷ The SciPy `pdist` function calculates the pair-wise distances between all of the submitted coordinates for the blobs.

❸ The NumPy `min` function then returns the minimum value of all of the calculated distances, and the `max` function returns the maximum value. The minimum value found is 40 and the max is 199.

These property functions are very good at helping answer questions about the features found in an image. Other examples include finding the largest or smallest object by area, objects that are the furthest to the left or right, and so on. These functions help categorize the features. They are also very useful for comparing a known object to an unknown object, a concept that will be covered in "Measuring Features" on page 185.

FeatureSet Sorting and Filtering

The final category of `FeatureSet` functions contains those that order or group features together, either by sorting the features or by filtering them down to a subset. The sorting functions sort the elements in a `FeatureSet` by comparing all of the individual features using a particular property. These properties should be familiar because many of the sorting functions work on the same properties covered in the previous section. These functions return a new `FeatureSet` in the sorted order. The functions include:

sortArea()
    Returns a new `FeatureSet` sorted with the features that have the smallest area first. By default, a `FeatureSet` is sorted by the area.

sortDistance()
    Returns a new `FeatureSet` sorted by the distance of each feature from a given coordinate (with the nearest listed first).

sortColorDistance()
    Returns a new `FeatureSet` where the features that are closest to a given color are listed first. If no color is provided, the function uses black as the comparison color. This then returns a `FeatureSet` where the features are sorted from darkest to lightest.

sortLength()
    Returns a new `FeatureSet` where the features with the greatest length are listed first.

```
sortAngle()
```
Returns a new FeatureSet where the features closest to a given angle are listed first. If no angle is given, the function compares the angles against the horizontal axis at 0.

The following example demonstrates how to sort objects by their color distance from blue. It also numbers the objects based on their distance. The object labeled with "1" is the closest to white, with each progressive number indicating less and less white.

```
from SimpleCV import Image

img = Image("colortiles.png")

tiles = img.binarize().findBlobs()

tiles.image = img

color_sorted_tiles = tiles.sortColorDistance(Color.BLUE)   ❶

count = 1   ❷

for tile in color_sorted_tiles:
    img.dl().text(str(count), tile.coordinates(), color = Color.RED)   ❸
    count += 1

img.show()
```

❶ This creates a new color_sorted_beans FeatureSet, where the colors are sorted by their distance from the color blue. The feature with the average color closest to blue is listed first.

❷ The count variable is used to show the order in which the colored tiles were listed in the color_sorted_beans FeatureSet.

❸ This prints the count number in red at the location of each tile.

The result looks like Figure 9-3, with the blue tile obviously being the closest to blue and the red tile being the furthest from it.

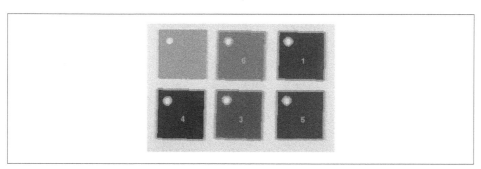

Figure 9-3. Detecting the objects that are closest to blue

While the SimpleCV framework has these standard FeatureSet sorting functions, it's also fairly simple to write a custom sort function. For example, the following code examines an image of several coins and finds the coin with the largest perimeter.

```
from SimpleCV import Image

img = Image("coins.png")

coins = img.binarize().findBlobs()

coins.image = img

perimeter_sorted = sorted(coins, key = lambda b: len(b.contour()))  ❶

perimeter_sorted[-1].draw(width=3)  ❷

img.show()
```

❶ This uses Python's built-in sorted() function to sort the coins FeatureSet using the length of each feature's contour or perimeter. To break this down a bit further, the key = lambda b: len(b.contour() portion of the code tells the sorted function to use a custom comparison function. The custom function it uses is then defined by Python's lambda keyword, which creates an anonymous function. The b is the argument for that anonymous function, and the function itself is defined by the expression that follows the :. In this case, that is the len(b.contour()) expression. All of this combined causes the sorted function to compare the contour lengths of each feature, and then return a list that is assigned to perimeter_sorted.

❷ The output of the previous line is a list sorted by the perimeter length, from the shortest to the longest perimeter. Use the -1 index to then get the largest in the list and draw it on the image.

Figure 9-4 shows the results, with the 50 cent coin correctly identified as the largest perimeter.

Figure 9-4. A 50 cent coin identified as having the largest perimeter

Whereas the sorting functions reorder the features by a given property, the filtering functions reduce the elements to a subset of the features that match a particular criteria. Each of the filter functions returns a new FeatureSet. The most useful of these functions is the `filter()` function itself. This function returns a FeatureSet that is filtered on a NumPy binary array. Since the property functions outlined above return NumPy arrays, they can be used as inputs in Python expressions to generate binary arrays. For instance, the following code creates a binary array of all of the features that have an area greater than or equal to 2,500 pixels:

```
from SimpleCV import Image

img = Image("coins.png")

blobs = img.binarize().findBlobs()

wide_blobs_binary_array = blobs.area() >= 2500  ❶
```

❶ The `wide_blobs_binary_array` will have a value of True for any blob whose width is greater than or equal to 2,500 pixels, and False for any blob whose width is less than 2,500 pixels.

With NumPy, binary arrays can also then be ANDed and ORed together, potentially creating more complex filter conditions. However, before diving into more complex examples, here is the full list of filtering methods:

`filter()`
> Returns a new FeatureSet of the features that match a particular criteria.

`inside()`
> Returns a new FeatureSet of the features found in a given region of an image.

`outside()`
> Returns a new FeatureSet of the features found outside a given region.

`overlaps()`
> Returns a new FeatureSet of the features that overlap a given region.

`above()`
> Returns a new FeatureSet of the features that are above a given region.

`below()`
> Returns a new FeatureSet of the features that are below a given region.

`left()`
> Returns a new FeatureSet of the features that are to the left of a given region.

`right()`
> Returns a new FeatureSet of the features that are to the right of a given region.

The following example code that uses the width information from the previous example to find just the larger coins:

```
from SimpleCV import Image

img = Image("coins.png")

blobs = img.binarize().findBlobs()

blobs.image = img

big_blobs_binary_array = blobs.area() >= 2500    ❶

big = blobs.filter(big_blobs_binary_array)    ❷

big.show(width=3)
```

❶ Filter the blobs, just like in the previous example.

❷ Pass the filter from the previous step as an argument to the `filter()` function. Note that this line could also be combined with the previous step to be: `big = blobs.fil ter(blobs.area() >= 2500)`

The result is demonstrated in Figure 9-5.

Figure 9-5. Coins with an area greater than 2,500 pixels are highlighted in green

The & (and) and | (or) operators can be combined to create more complex filters. For example, the nickles in the coins image are between 2,500 and 2,600 pixels in area. To find only the nickels:

```
from SimpleCV import Image
import numpy as np

img = Image("coins.png")

blobs = img.binarize().findBlobs()

blobs.image = img

nickels = blobs.filter((blobs.area() > 2500) &  (blobs.area() < 2600))    ❶

nickels.show(width=3)
```

❶ This creates a new `FeatureSet` where each feature has an area that is both greater than 2,500 and less than 2,600 pixels. The result is demonstrated in Figure 9-6.

Figure 9-6. The nickels found in the coins image

 When combining filter criteria, make sure that it does not filter all possible conditions. For example, an easy typo in the example to find nickels is to look for objects with an area greater than 2,600 and less than 2,500 pixels. Obviously this condition cannot exist, so no results would be returned.

Cropping FeatureSets

In many cases, the detected feature is not the end goal. Instead, it may be an interim step for finding the actual desired object. For example, the first step could be to find a package in an image. Then the second step is to find the barcode on the package. In other words, step one is to crop the image to just the part with a package, and then perform a second feature detection. Not surprisingly, the function to crop an image around a feature is named `crop()` . The `crop()` function, when called on a feature, will frame each feature with a bounding box, which is the smallest rectangle possible that would still contain all of the pixels with the feature in it. If the feature has an irregular shape or is rotated, the cropped image will still contain some "background" pixels.

Figure 9-7 shows the link between the shape of an image and its bounding box. It represents a common tape dispenser. Because it has curved edges and a hole in the middle, the bounding box also encapsulates part of the background.

When calling the `crop()` method on a `FeatureSet`, the function returns an array of cropped image objects (one image for each feature in the set). The following example demonstrates how to count pills in a pack, such as in Figure 9-8. It searches for the bubbles of the pill pack, crops down to just that bubble, and then searches for pills in those bubbles.

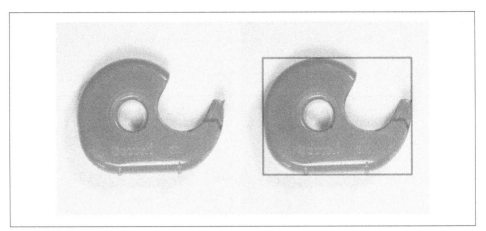

Figure 9-7. A bounding box around a tape dispenser

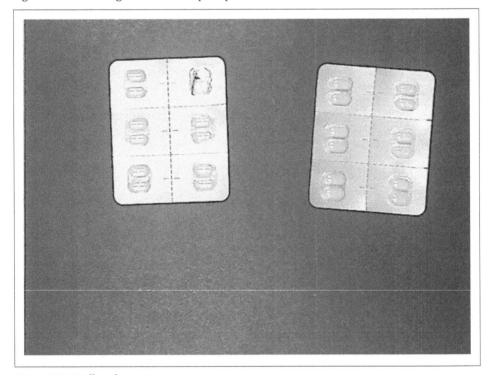

Figure 9-8. A pill pack

```
from SimpleCV import Image

pill_image = Image("pills.png")

packs = pill_image.findBlobs()
```

```
pack_images = packs.crop()   ❶

pill_color = (149, 189, 198)   ❷

for individual_pack in pack_images:

    hue_distance = individual_pack.hueDistance(pill_color, 50, 80)   ❸

    pill_count = len(hue_distance.invert().findBlobs(minsize = 100))   ❹

    print "This pack has %d pills." % pill_count   ❺
```

❶ The `crop()` function returns an image for each blob found in the image.

❷ When searching for the pills in the pill packs, it will search for blobs that are a particular "pill blue" color. This is the RGB triplet for that particular blue color.

❸ Use the `hueDistance` to look for things that are "pill blue". The additional arguments passed here make sure that only items sufficiently blue and sufficiently bright are included. The values for these arguments were found with a little bit of hand tuning and trial and error.

❹ The `len()` function is a built-in function in Python that returns the length of a list. In this case, it computes the number of blue blobs found, which is also the number of pills found in each pack.

❺ This line uses Python's format operator to format the string to be printed. The format operator follows a form or "format % value". When there is a % in the format string, the corresponding value will be substituted in for it. In this case, the `%d` tells Python that the value that will be substituted in is an integer, and the value itself is `pill_count`.

The preceding code prints the following:

```
This pack has 12 pills.
This pack has 10 pills.
```

This demonstrates one of the most useful applications with cropping features—detecting features within features with relative ease.

Measuring Features

Blobs and other features frequently have amorphous shapes and sizes that might make measurements a little more challenging. However, there are a variety of different approaches for measuring features—even when they are not in the form of simple geometric shapes. Some of these measurements include:

`topLeftCorner()`
    Returns the (X, Y) tuple for the upper left corner of the bounding box

`topRightCorner()`
    Returns the (X, Y) tuple for the upper right corner of the bounding box

`bottomRightCorner()`
    Returns the (X, Y) tuple for the lower right corner of the bounding box

`bottomLeftCorner()`
    Returns the (X, Y) tuple for the lower left corner of the bounding box

`minX()`
    Returns the smallest X coordinate of the bounding box

`maxX()`
    Returns the largest X coordinate of the bounding box

`minY()`
    Returns the smallest Y coordinate of the bounding box

`maxY()`
    Returns the largest Y coordinate of the bounding box

`center()`
    Returns the (X, Y) coordinates for the center of the bounding box

`width()`
    Returns the width of the bounding box

`height()`
    Returns the height of the bounding box

The idea of a bounding rectangle was discussed in the previous section. The minimum bounding rectangle is similar to the bounding box rectangle except that it's not constrained to have horizontal or vertical sides. Instead, the minimum rectangle is the smallest rectangle possible to encapsulate the blob, which usually means that it is rotated in order to have the closest fit. Because the minimum rectangle is a closer fit to the actual blob, it has more accurate information about a blob's dimensions. An example of a minimum bounding rectangle is shown below:

```
from SimpleCV import Image

img = Image('lightbolt.png')

blobs = img.binarize().findBlobs()

blobs.image = img

blobs[0].drawMinRect()  ❶

img.show()
```

Notice that unlike a regular bounding rectangle, which would have edges square to the sides of the windows, this bounding rectangle is rotated to encapsulate the lightning bolt in the smallest possible rectangle, as demonstrated in Figure 9-9.

Not surprisingly, the minimum rectangle has data associated with it that is similar to that of the bounding box. One word of caution, though: sometimes the interpretation

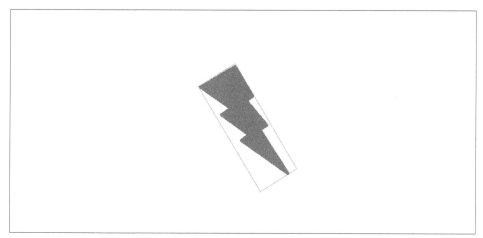

Figure 9-9. Blob with a minimum bounding rectangle

for these data points is slightly different than that of the bounding box. Here are the methods that return data for the minimum rectangle:

getMinRectPoints()
> Returns a list of (X, Y) tuples that represent the corners of the minimum rectangle

angle()
> Returns the angle between the x-axis and the blob's minimum rectangle

minRectX()
> Returns the X coordinate of the center of the minimum rectangle

minRectY()
> Returns the Y coordinate of the geometric center of the minimum rectangle

minRectWidth()
> Returns the width of the minimum rectangle

minRectHeight()
> Returns the height of the minimum rectangle

In addition to working with bounding rectangles, it is also possible to do several basic computations with the feature itself. This information includes:

area()
> Computes the area of the blob in terms of the number of pixels included in the contour of the blob

centroid()
> Returns the centroid, or geometric center, of the blob

contour()
> Returns a list of all of the (X ,Y) coordinates of the points on the outer perimeter of the blob

`radius()`

Returns the average distance between the centroid and every point on the contour of the blob

`isCircle()`

Checks to see if the blob is in the shape of a circle, and returns True or False

`isRectangle()`

Checks to see if the blob is in the shape of a rectangle, and returns True or False

`isSquare()`

Checks to see if the blob is in the shape of a square, and returns True or False

But enough with the listing of measurement functions for blobs. The best way to learn about measurement in terms of blobs is to see it in action. This is demonstrated in the next section.

Quarter for Scale

As was first introduced in Chapter 4, a common vision system application is to use the size of a known object to measure the size of an unknown object. This example shows how a quarter, which has a known size, can be used to compute the size of a USB drive. The general theme for this code is as follows:

1. Start with a quarter, which was previously measured to have a diameter of 24.26 mm.
2. Find the size in pixels of the quarter in an image.
3. Using the above, find the ratio of pixels to millimeters.
4. Find the size in pixels of the USB drive.
5. Use the previously computed ratio of pixels to millimeters to translate the number of pixels for the USB drive into its dimensions in millimeters.

```
from SimpleCV import Image

# A quarter has a diameter of 24.26 mm
quarter_size = 24.26

# This holds the ratio of the image size to a quarter's actual size
size_ratio = 0
object_size = 0

img = Image('quarter.png')

bin = img.colorDistance(Color.GRAY).invert().binarize(200).morphClose()

blobs = bin.findBlobs()   ❶

circles = blobs.filter([b.isCircle() for b in blobs])   ❷
```

```
    if circles:
        quarter = circles[-1]  ❸
        diameter = quarter.radius() * 2  ❹
        size_ratio = diameter / quarter_size  ❺

    rectangles = blobs.filter([b.isRectangle() for b in blobs])  ❻

    if rectangles:
        usb_drive = rectangles[-1]
        usb_width = usb_drive.width() / size_ratio
        usb_height = usb_drive.height() / size_ratio

        print "USB drive is " + (str(usb_width)) + " mm wide and "
            + (str(usb_height)) + " mm tall"  ❼
```

❶ The first step is to find blobs that represent the quarter and the USB drive from the original image.

❷ The findBlobs() function should find two blobs. The next step is to figure out which of the blobs is the quarter. Since we know the circular object is the quarter, we use the filter() function to filter the set of blobs to only circles. We identify the circles by using the isCircle() function.

❸ The set of circular blobs is sorted according to size. Selecting index [-1] from this array returns the largest circle, which should be the quarter.

❹ Because the quarter is circular, we can use the radius function to find its overall diameter. We could also use the width or height of the bounding box, as this should roughly be equivalent.

❺ This calculates the ratio of pixel size to actual size in millimeters. We use this later to convert the width of the USB drive, as measured in pixels, to millimeters.

❻ The USB drive is rectangular, so we filter the blobs with the isRectangle() function to find the rectangular blobs.

❼ Finally, using the previously computed size_ratio and the height and width of the USB drive in pixels, we print out the size of the USB drive in millimeters. It reports that the drive measures 21mm×67mm, after rounding.

Blobs and Convex Hulls

A convex hull, also referred to as a convex envelope, is the smallest convex polygon that can surround a blob. The middle school math definition of convex just means that something is curved outward and has no indentations, much like a balloon. (Mathematicians have a more formal definition, but the simple definition is good enough for this book.) The easiest way to think about a convex hull, however, is to think about a rubber band wrapped around an object. If there are any indentations in the blob, the rubber band won't move in to follow the surface of the blob. Instead, it will follow a straight line to the next outwardly facing point in the blob. For example, Figure 9-10 shows the convex hull drawn around a tape dispenser.

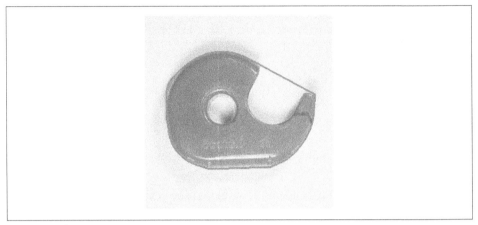

Figure 9-10. A convex hull around a tape dispenser

Within the SimpleCV framework, the convex hull of a blob is drawn using the function `drawHull()`. As an example, the following code draws the convex hull around a wooden puzzle:

```
from SimpleCV import Image

img = Image("puzzle.png")

blobs = img.binarize().findBlobs()

blobs.image = img

blobs[-1].drawHull(color=Color.RED)  ❶

img.show()
```

❶ This draws the red convex hull onto the original version of the image.

The resulting image will appear like the image on the right in Figure 9-11, with the hull looking like a diamond-like shape pointing downwards.

 Blobs also have a variable called `mConvexHull` that stores the contour points of the convex hull as a set of (X, Y) tuples.

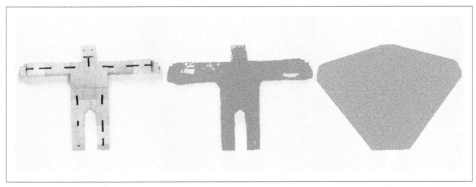

Figure 9-11. Left: The original puzzle; Center: Blob detection; Right: The convex hull

Inside a Blob

Blobs are not always a solid set of pixels. Sometimes there are empty spaces within the blob, which are called holes. Within those holes, there can sometimes be other blobs or islands, and within those islands there can be more holes, and so on and so on. In the SimpleCV framework, whenever blobs are found, the blob object will also have a list of all of its holes, if any.

The following example finds the hole in a tape dispenser:

```
from SimpleCV import

img = Image('tape.png')

blobs = img.binarize().morphClose().findBlobs()   ❶

blobs.image = img

blobs[-1].drawHoles()   ❷

img.show()
```

❶ Note that this example also uses a `morphClose()`. When doing the blog detection, it actually has a lot of little holes that are insignificant. To clean those up, use a basic morph.

❷ Now draw the holes using the `drawHoles()` function.

The output from the code is demonstrated in Figure 9-12. Notice that it found the main hole in the middle of the dispenser and a false positive hole from a bright reflection on the bottom of the dispenser.

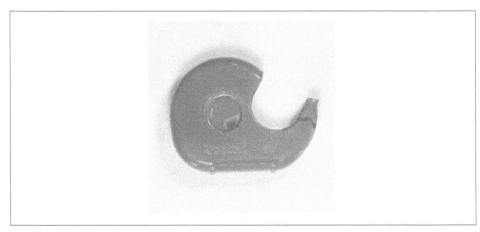

Figure 9-12. Holes in the blob of the tape dispenser

Rotating Blobs

Frequently, a blob will be rotated in an image and need to be straightened out to make it easier to work with. There are two functions to help with this. The first is a straight-forward `rotate()` function, which takes as a required argument the number of degrees to rotate the blob. It works just like the image rotation functions discussed in Chapter 4. It works well for basic rotation tasks, but sometimes can require fine-tuning to determine the correct degree of rotation.

There is a second function that solves this problem, and the function itself estimates the best angle to rotate the object. It's called `rectifyMajorAxis()`. It finds the longest side of the minimum rectangle for the blob, and then rotates the blob so that the longest side is then parallel to the x-axis. This is particularly useful when comparing the same object across many different images, and the object may be shifting its orientation in each image. It's also useful when comparing two or more of the same types of objects in an image, as the objects might not be nicely aligned to one another. Note, however, that this function is not the silver bullet of rotation. The first issue is that if the blob is perfectly round, this method won't work. The second is that while the function can identify the longest side of the box, it can't tell which side is "up". When it aligns the blob, it could put the blob upside down or on its side.

For example, the following code will rectify the lightning bolt image used in previous examples:

```
from SimpleCV import Image

img = Image('lightbolt.png')

blobs = img.binarize().findBlobs()   ❶

blobs[-1].rectifyMajorAxis()   ❷
```

```
corrected = blobs[-1].getBlobImage()   ❸

corrected.show()
```

❶ Find the blobs, just like in other examples.

❷ Call the `rectifyMajorAxis()` function on the largest blob found. The largest blob is the lightning bolt, and rectifying it essentially lays it on its side.

❸ Once it is rectified, the revised blob image is extracted using the `getBlobImage()` function.

The output is demonstrated in Figure 9-13.

Figure 9-13. The lightning bolt image laid on its side

Example: Tracking a Circle (Ball)

This example demonstrates how to track a ball or other circular object on the screen. One important point of this example is that it keeps track of the previously found circle and then uses that information to find the same object in the next frame of the video. Although there are more robust ways to accomplish object tracking with computer vision, this example provides a basic and simple introduction on how to use the previous information in the current image to determine if it the same object or not.

```
from SimpleCV import Camera, Color, Display

cam = Camera()
disp = Display()

previous_ball_xy = None
previous_ball_size = 100

while disp.isNotDone():
    img = cam.getImage()

    dist = img.colorDistance(Color.BLACK).dilate(2)   ❶
    segmented = dist.binarize()
    blobs = segmented.findBlobs(minsize=2000)
```

```
if blobs:
    circles = blobs.filter([b.isCircle(0.2) for b in blobs])  ❷
    if circles:
        if previous_ball_xy:  ❸
            fcircles = circles.filter([c.radius() >
                (previous_ball_size * 0.5) for c in circles])  ❹
            distances = [int(c.distanceFrom(previous_ball_xy))
                for c in fcircles]  ❺
            nearest = blobs[distances.index(min(distances))]  ❻
            img.drawCircle((nearest.x, nearest.y), nearest.radius(),
                Color.RED, thickness=4)  ❼
            previous_ball_xy = (nearest.x, nearest.y)
            previous_ball_size = nearest.radius()
        else:
            previous_ball_xy = (circles[-1].x, circles[-1].y)
            previous_ball_size = circles[-1].radius()
    else:
        img.drawText("No circles found")
img.save(disp)
```

❶ This first step assumes that the ball is black—or at least a dark color—and performs a segmentation based on black. Obviously, this should be changed if looking for a different colored ball.

❷ This is the first filter, which looks for only circular blob objects.

❸ This is just a test to see if a ball was found previously. If not, the first match is merely recorded. If a ball was previously found, then it is used to help identify the ball in the current frame.

❹ The next filter looks at the radius of the ball. It will only consider balls that are at least half the size of the previous ball.

❺ Next, compute the distance between any currently found balls and the ball found the last time, which will be used in the next filter.

❻ We are going to assume that the ball will not move much between frames. So the ball that is closest is most likely the same ball as from the previous frame.

❼ Draw a red line around the ball.

An example of the output is demonstrated in Figure 9-14. Granted, that is not a ball in the picture, it is a circle drawn on a piece of paper. But it shows how the image successfully identified the circle and outlined it in red.

Figure 9-14. Tracking the black dot as it moves across the screen

Advanced Features

Chapter 9 introduced feature detection and extraction, but mostly focused on common geometric shapes like lines and circles. Even blobs assume that there is a contiguous grouping of similar pixels. This chapter builds on those results by looking for more complex objects. Most of this detection is performed by searching for a template of a known form in a larger image. This chapter also provides an overview of optical flow, which attempts to identify objects that change between two frames. The specific topics for this chapter include:

- Finding instances of template images in a larger image
- Using Haar classifiers, particularly to identify faces
- Barcode scanning for 1D and 2D barcodes
- Finding keypoints, which is a more robust form of template matching
- Tracking objects that move

Bitmap Template Matching

As the name implies, this algorithm works by searching for instances where a bitmap template—a small image of the object to be found—can be found within a larger image. For example, if trying to create a vision system to play Where's Waldo, the template image would be a picture of Waldo. To match his most important feature, his face, the Waldo template would be cropped to right around his head and include a minimal amount of the background. A template with his whole body would only match instances where his whole body was visible and positioned exactly the same way. The other component in template matching is the image to be searched. In the Waldo example, this would be the picture of all the distracting objects and people. The image being searched always needs to be larger than the template image for there to be a match.

Although this approach supports searching for a wide variety of different objects, it can still be a fickle friend. This method is *not* scale or rotation invariant, which means the size of the object in the template must equal the size it is in the image. Lighting conditions also can have an impact because the image brightness or the reflection on specular objects can stop a match from being found. Even a clean match on a rotated version of the object can create challenges. As a result, the matching works best when used in an extremely controlled environment.

The template matching feature works by calling the `findTemplate()` function on the `Image` object to be searched. Next, pass as a parameter the template of the object to be found. Using the Where's Waldo example, if the image to search is called `TheBigPicture`, and the template image of Waldo's face is called `Waldo`, the syntax for the template match would be `TheBigPicture.findTemplate(Waldo)`. The example below demonstrates this process by looking for the black pieces on a Go board. The first piece of the example is a Go board, such as the one shown in Figure 10-1.

Figure 10-1. Pieces on a Go board

Figure 10-2 is the template image for a black piece. Notice that it is cropped tightly around the piece so that it essentially looks like a black square. However, it is hard to see, but there is a slight variance in color that corresponds to the light reflecting off the black piece. Under different lighting conditions, this would cause there to be no matches.

Figure 10-2. Template of black piece

```
from SimpleCV import Image

# Get the template and image
goBoard = Image('go.png')
black = Image('go-black.png')

# Find the matches and draw them
matches = goBoard.findTemplate(black)   ❶
matches.draw()   ❷

# Show the board with matches print the number
goBoard.show()
```

```
print str(len(matches)) + " matches found."
# Should output: 9 matches found.
```

❶ In this case, `black` is the template image, which is a cropped version of a single, black Go piece. The goBoard is the image of the Go board with the pieces on it.

❷ The draw function draws a box around each match. The match is a little off center on one piece, but otherwise, the matching caught the nine black pieces on the board, as you can see in Figure 10-3.

Figure 10-3. Matches for black pieces

The `findTemplate()` function also takes two optional arguments: method and threshold. The `method` argument defines the algorithm to use for the matching, and the threshold argument fine-tunes the quality of the matches. Details about the various available matching algorithms can by found by typing `help Image.findTemplate` in the SimpleCV shell. The `threshold` option works like thresholds with other feature matching functions, where decreasing the threshold results in more matches, but could also result in more false positives. These tuning parameters can help the quality of results, but template matching is error prone in all but the most controlled, consistent environments. Keypoint matching, which is described in the next section, is a more robust approach.

Keypoint Template Matching

Tracking an object as it moves between two images is a hard problem for a computer vision system. This is a challenge that requires identifying an object in one image, finding that same object in the second image, and then computing the amount of movement. Earlier chapters have demonstrated how to detect that something has changed in an image, using techniques such as subtracting one image from another. While the feature detectors we've looked at so far are useful for identifying objects in a single image, they are often sensitive to different degrees of rotation or variable lighting conditions. As these are both common issues when tracking an object in motion, a more robust feature extractor is needed.

One solution is to use keypoints. A *keypoint* describes an object in terms that are independent of position, rotation, and lighting. For example, in many environments, detecting corners make good keypoints. As described in Chapter 8, a corner is made from two intersecting lines at any angle. Move a corner from the top-left to the bottom-right of the screen and the angle between the two intersecting lines remains the same. Rotate the image, and the angle remains the same. Shine more light on the corner, and it's still the same angle. Scale the image to twice its size, and again, the angle remains the same. Corners are robust to many environmental conditions and image transformations. Keypoints can be more than just corners, but corners provide an intuitive framework for understudying the underpinnings of keypoint detection.

The keypoints are extracted using the `findKeypoints()` function from the `Image` library. In addition to the typical feature properties, such as size and location, a keypoint also has a `descriptor()` function that outputs the actual points that are robust to location, rotation, scale, and so on. The following block of code demonstrates a basic application of keypoints by looking for keypoint features on the hotel keycard shown in Figure 10-4.

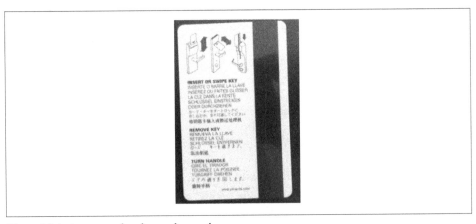

Figure 10-4. A common hotel room keycard

```
from SimpleCV import Image

card = Image('keycard.png')
keys = card.findKeypoints()    ❶

keys.draw()    ❷

card.show()
```

❶ Find the keypoints on the image using the `findKeypoints()` method.

❷ Draw those keypoints on the screen. They will appear as green circles at each point. The size of the circle represents the quality of the keypoint.

Figure 10-5 shows the resulting keypoints with this typical hotel room keycard.

The above keypoints are not particularly valuable on their own, but the next step is to apply this concept to perform template matching. As with the `findTemplate()` ap-

Figure 10-5. The extracted keypoints

proach, a template image is used to find keypoint matches. However, unlike the previous example, keypoint matching does not work directly off the template image. Instead, the process extracts the keypoints from the template image, and then looks for those keypoints in the target image. This results in a much more robust matching system.

Although keypoints begin to address the limitations of previous template matching tools, they do have limitations. Keypoint matching works best when the object has a lot of texture with diverse colors and shapes. Objects with uniform color and simple shapes do not have enough keypoints to find good matches. In addition, the matching works best with small rotations, usually less than 45 degrees. Greater or larger rotations could work, but it will be harder for the algorithm to find a match.

Whereas the `findTemplate()` function looks for multiple matches of the template, the `findKeypointMatch()` function returns only the best match for the template. The `find KeypointMatch()` function is called on the `Image` to be searched and takes four arguments:

`template` *(required)*
    The template image to search for in the target image.

`quality`
    Configures the quality threshold for matches. By default, it is 500. Values between 300 and 500 tend to work best.

`minDist`
    The minimum distance between two feature vectors necessary in order to treat them as a match. The lower the value, the better the quality. Too low a value, though, prevents good matches from being returned. The default is 0.2, with values in the range from 0.05 to 0.3 returning the best results in most circumstances.

minMatch

> The minimum percentage of feature matches that must be found to match an object with the template. The default value is 0.4 (40%), and good values typically range from 0.3 to 0.7.

Would you like to see the keypoint matches between the two images? The drawKey pointMatches() function shows a side-by-side image, with lines drawn between the two images to indicate where it finds a match. An example is demonstrated in Figure 10-6. This is a good way to diagnose issues with matching. If it draws lots of matches, the matching algorithm should work. If it draws no lines or very few, then there may be problems performing the match.

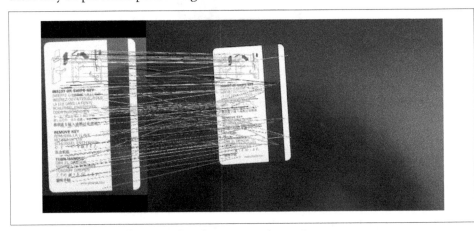

Figure 10-6. The lines indicate matching keypoints on the two images

The example below uses a template image of a keycard—based on the previous example —to identify the same card sitting on a table. The results are demonstrated in Figure 10-7.

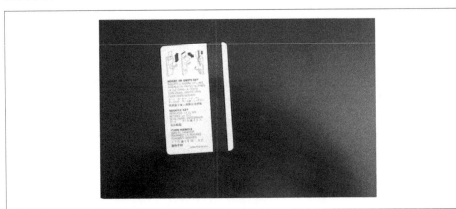

Figure 10-7. Keycard sitting on the table

```
from SimpleCV import Image

template = Image('ch10-card.png')  ❶

img = Image('ch10-card-on-table.png')

match = img.findKeypointMatch(template)  ❷

match.draw(width=3)  ❸

img.show()
```

❶ This is the picture of the keycard. It is the template for the keypoints that will be searched for in the card-on-table image.

❷ Search for keypoint matches with the `findKeypointMatch()` function. Pass this function an image of the object for which to search. It automatically detects the keypoints and uses them to perform the match.

❸ Next, draw a box around the detected object. Note that keypoint matching only finds the single best match for the image. If multiple keycards were on the table, it would only report the closest match.

The result looks like Figure 10-8.

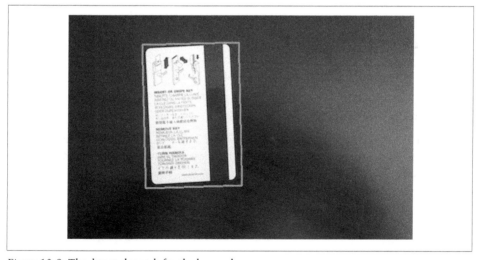

Figure 10-8. The detected match for the keycard

Optical Flow

The next logical step beyond template matching is to understand how to track objects between frames. Optical flow is very similar to template matching in that it takes a small area of one image and then scans the same region in a second image in an attempt to find a match. If a match is found, the system indicates the direction of travel, as measured in (X, Y) points.

 Only the two-dimensional travel distance is recorded. If the object also moved closer to or further away from the camera, this distance is not recorded.

Optical flow in the SimpleCV framework is computed with the findMotion() function. This function has a single required parameter, previous_frame, which is the image used for comparison. The previous frame must be the same size. In addition, for purposes of computing direction of motion, it assumes that the previous_frame occurs before the current image (as implied by the name "previous_frame"). In other words, given two images named imageAtTimeOne and imageAtTimeTwo, to find the movement between them use: imageAtTimeTwo.findMotion(imageAtTimeOne). To see this in action:

```
from SimpleCV import Camera, Color, Display

cam = Camera()

previous = cam.getImage()   ❶

disp = Display(previous.size())

while not disp.isDone():
    current = cam.getImage()   ❷
    motion = current.findMotion(previous)   ❸
    for m in motion:
        m.draw(color=Color.RED,normalize=False)   ❹

    current.save(disp)
    previous = current   ❺
```

❶ To find any movement, it will need to have both a previous and a current image to compare. These images are updated in the loop, but we need an initial previous image to kick off the process.

❷ With each iteration through the loop, capture a new image to serve as the current image.

❸ Find the objects that have moved by comparing the current image to the previous image.

❹ Draw the little red motion lines on the screen to indicate where the motion occurred.

❺ Finally, replace the old previous image for the next iteration through the loop.

Figure 10-9 is an example of the motion detection output. The red lines indicate where the motion occurred.

Figure 10-9. Optical flow example

 The findMotion function supports several different algorithms to detect motion. For additional information, type help Image to look up the findMotion() documentation in the SimpleCV shell, or see *http://sim plecv.org/docs*.

Haar-like Features

Unlike template matching, Haar-like Features are used to classify more generic objects. They are particularly popular for face detection, where the system determines whether an object is a generic face. This is different from face recognition, which tries to identify whose face is in the image and is a much more complicated process. Simply knowing that an object is a face is useful for segmenting the image, narrowing down a region of interest, or simply doing some other fun tricks.

Technically, Haar-like features refer to a way of slicing and dicing an image to identify the key patterns. The template information is stored in a file known as a Haar Cascade, usually formatted as an XML file. This requires a fair amount of work to train a classifier system and generate the cascade file. Fortunately, the SimpleCV framework includes some common face detection cascades, and additional ones are available on the Internet. The built-in cascades with the SimpleCV framework include:

- Forward-looking faces
- Profile faces
- Eyes
- Noses
- Mouths
- Ears
- Upper and lower bodies

 Appendix C covers more details on using Haar-like features for matching other types of objects.

Like the template matching described in the previous section, Haar Cascades also work
best in controlled environments. For example, the Haar Cascade for detecting forward-
looking faces will not work well on an image with a face looking to the side. Size and
rotation of the object can also create complications, though the underlying algorithms
are more flexible than with template matching.

Haar-like features are detected with the `findHaarFeatures()` function of the `Image`
library. It takes four parameters:

cascade
> The path the Haar Cascade `XML` file.

scale_factor
> The Haar Cascades are technically sensitive to the image's scale. To simulate scale
> invariance, the algorithm is run multiple times, scaling the template up with each
> run. The amount that the template should be scaled is controlled by the
> `scale_factor`. Under the default factor of 1.2, it scales up the template 20% each
> time.

min_neighbors
> This is like a threshold value in other feature detectors. Technically, it deals with
> the number of adjacent detections needed to classify the object, but conceptually
> it is easier to think of as a threshold parameter. The default value is 2.

use_canny
> The default value is to use Canny pruning to reduce false positives in potentially
> noisy images. This is usually always the best option.

The following example identifies the face of a user looking at the camera (see Figure 10-10).

```
from SimpleCV import Camera, Display

cam = Camera()
```

Figure 10-10. Face detection, as represented by the green box

```
disp = Display(cam.getImage().size())

while disp.isNotDone():
    img = cam.getImage()

    # Look for a face
    faces = img.findHaarFeatures('face')   ❶

    if faces is not None:
        # Get the largest face
        faces = faces.sortArea()
        bigFace = faces[-1]

        # Draw a green box around the face
        bigFace.draw()

    img.save(disp)
```

❶ This loads one of the built-in Haar Cascade files. If working with a Haar Cascade that was downloaded from the Internet or created manually, simply specify the full path to the file. The detection works like most other feature detectors. Simply pass the cascade file loaded earlier and it returns a FeatureSet with the matches.

Barcode

One-dimensional barcodes have become a ubiquitous part of the modern shopping experience, and two-dimensional barcodes are becoming increasingly popular for storing contact information, URL's, and other small bits of information. This growing popularity is helped by the availability of open source tools that can be used to extract information from these barcodes. One example of these tools is the ZXing library (pronounced "Zebra Crossing"), which is an image processing library for barcodes. The SimpleCV framework works with the ZXing library, making it easy to process images of one- and two-dimensional barcodes as part of a vision system.

 As of SimpleCV version 1.3, ZXing is not automatically installed. If it is not installed, trying to use the barcode functions will throw a warning and not work. For instructions on installing ZXing, type `help Image.findBarcode` from the SimpleCV shell, or go to *http://code.google.com/p/zxing/*.

To extract the information from a barcode, use the `findBarcode()` function. It works with both one-dimensional and two-dimensional barcodes. The image to be scanned can contain more than just a barcode, but the detector works best when there is not a lot of extra noise around it. In addition, while most barcodes are designed to work in spite of a partial obstruction of the barcode, the detector works best when it has a clear view of the barcode.

```
from SimpleCV import Image, Barcode

# Load a one-dimensional barcode
img = Image('upc.png')

barcode = img.findBarcode()   ❶

print barcode.data   ❷
# Should output: 987654321098
```

❶ Call the `findBarcode()` function to extract the relevant information. In this case, it is an image with only a one-dimensional barcode (see Figure 10-11). Store the result in `barcode`.

❷ The `data` property contains the data from the barcode.

This works just as well with a Quick Response (or QR) code, such as the one in Figure 10-12.

```
from SimpleCV import Image, Barcode

# Load a QR barcode
img = Image('qr.png')

barcode = img.findBarcode()
```

Figure 10-11. Example of a one-dimensional barcode

```
print barcode.data.rstrip()
# Should output: http://www.simplecv.org
```

Note that the `findBarcode` function does both a detection and data extraction process in one go, thanks to the way ZXing works. There is no need to first detect if an object is a barcode and then extract the encoded information.

Figure 10-12. Example of a QR barcode

Examples

The examples section for this chapter covers some slightly more in-depth applications for the concepts in this chapter. The following examples are included:

- A barcode scanner that is handy for reading everything from QR codes to the two-dimensional barcode on a library book.

- A mustacheinator that uses the Haar feature detector to find a face and draw a mustache on it.

Barcode Scanner

This example works like the basic barcode code from earlier in the chapter, except that now it is designed to read barcodes from the camera. Because the barcode detection is somewhat computationally expensive, it may be necessary to hold the barcode in front of the camera for a few seconds. This example works best when the barcode is the dominant item on the screen.

 Want to generate a QR code for use in this example? Search the Internet for "QR Code Generator" to get a list of free websites for generating QR codes. Generate a code, print it, and hold it in front of the camera.

```
from SimpleCV import Color, Camera, Display

cam = Camera()
display = Display()

message = "Last item scanned: "
result = "None"

while( display.isNotDone() ):
    img = cam.getImage()

    barcode = img.findBarcode()    ❶
    if( barcode is not None ):
        result = str(barcode.data)    ❷

    img.drawText(message + result, color=Color.GREEN, fontsize=40)

    img.save(display)
```

❶ Find the barcode. This is a simple matter of calling the `findBarcode()` function. If no barcode is detected, it returns `None`.

❷ The results of the barcode scan are held in the **data** field of the barcode object.

The example image was taken with a QR barcode containing the following URL: *http://www.simplecv.org*, as is shown in Figure 10-13.

Figure 10-13. An example from the barcode reader; in the right figure, the contents of the barcode are shown in the upper-left corner

Mustacheinator

This example uses face detection to draw a mustache on the largest face found in the image from the camera. It works in a two-step process, by first identifying a face on the larger image, and then detecting a nose on the previously identified face. After that, most of the work is computing the coordinates for drawing the mustache.

```
from SimpleCV import Camera, Display, Image

cam = Camera()
disp = Display(cam.getImage().size())

# Load the stache and alpha mask
stache = Image("mustache.png")
mask = stache.createAlphaMask()    ❶

while disp.isNotDone():
    img = cam.getImage()

    faces = img.findHaarFeatures('face')   ❷
    if( faces is not None ):
        # Get the biggest face
        face = faces.sortArea()[-1]
        myface = face.crop()   ❸

        noses = myface.findHaarFeatures('nose')   ❹
        # If we have a nose
        if( noses is not None ):
            nose = noses.sortArea()[-1]

            # Calculate the mustache position
            xmust = face.points[0][0] + nose.x + (stache.width/2)   ❺
            ymust = face.points[0][1] + nose.y +(2*nose.height()/3)
```

```
# Blit the stache/mask onto the image
img = img.blit(stache,pos=(xmust,ymust), mask=mask)  ❻
```

```
img.save(disp)
```

❶ The mustache image must be transparent so that only the mustache portion appears, and not the white border around the mustache.

❷ First, find the face. This is the face on which the mustache will be drawn. It is easier to get a good match for a nose if the region is limited first to a face.

❸ Crop the image down to just the face.

❹ Next, do the nose detection on the face image.

❺ Because the nose was detected on the face image, the coordinates are relative to the face image. These next lines of code then use the position of the face image to translate those coordinates into the appropriate position of the overall picture. Note that `points` corresponds to the upper left corner of the face, and `nose.x` and `nose.y` correspond to the center point of the nose.

❻ Finally, draw the mustache on the image.

Figure 10-14 shows an author enjoying the benefits of the Mustacheinator code.

Figure 10-14. A fine looking stache

Advanced Shell Tips

Chapter 2 introduced the SimpleCV shell and some of the most common commands. This appendix covers a few additional tricks for working with the shell, including:

- Macros to automate tasks
- Timing to test the performance on scripts

Not all vision system developers need to know this, but power users may find that these tricks help streamline the development process.

Macro Magic

Chapter 2 described the SimpleCV shell as a tool for testing small snippets of code. However, when working with more than a few lines of code, it is often convenient to create reusable blocks of code. This is done with macros. Macro means big. In the case of a shell, this means a big block of code. Obviously, big is a relative term, in this case contrasted with the "micro" size of a few lines of code. Macros are most appropriate when testing or using the same block of code repeatedly. For example, macros are great for automatically setting up the camera object, loading a few images, or other repetitive initialization tasks.

 Macros probably sound a bit like functions. However, macros do not take any parameters. The closest thing to a parameter with a macro is to create variables outside of the macro, set those variables to a desired value, and then reference those variables from inside the macro.

The SimpleCV shell already has macro support built in. Shell macros are created from the history of previously used commands. These commands are bundled together into a single macro. A macro can be thought of as a shortcut versus using the up-arrow to look up and execute a bunch of previously entered commands. Therefore, the first step in constructing the macro is to run the commands to be included in the macro. For example, in the SimpleCV shell, perform the following basic camera setup:

```
>>> from SimpleCV import Camera
>>> cam = Camera()
>>> img = cam.getImage()
```

Notice that each line of code entered in the shell has a line number associated with it. For example, the first line of code is labeled with `SimpleCV:1`. The previously entered example should look like Figure A-1.

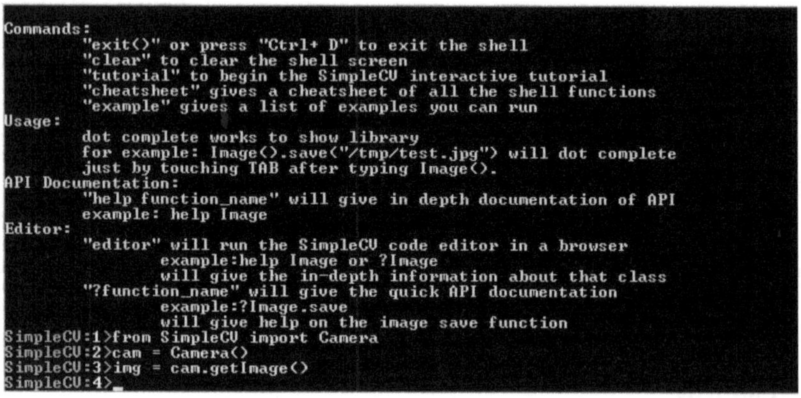

Figure A-1. Notice the line numbering for each shell command

Although the line numbers for the commands are displayed in the SimpleCV prompt, the commands are interlaced with the output of those commands. However, on most systems, the `history` function lists all previous commands and their line number.

```
>>> history  ❶
1: from SimpleCV import Camera  ❷
2: cam = Camera()
3: img = cam.getImage()
4: _ip.magic("history ")
```

❶ Enter the history command to output the list of previous commands.

❷ The following will be output, showing the previous commands.

Your actual line numbers may vary from the above description if you issued other commands during your shell session. However, the overall format should look similar. In particular, you should see the previously entered commands to initialize the camera and snap a picture. The next step is to create a macro to easily initialize the camera and grab a picture. In our example, the commands involved correspond to the line numbers 1 through 3. To create the macro, use the `macro` command with the name to give the new marcro and the appropriate line numbers to include in the macro. For example, to create a macro named *quickinit*, and have it execute the commands from lines 1 through 3:

```
>>> macro quickinit 1-3 ❶
Macro `quickinit` created. To execute, type its name (without quotes). ❷
Macro contents:
from SimpleCV import Camera
cam = Camera()
img = cam.getImage()
```

❶ Enter the word `macro`, followed by the name of the macro and the line numbers to include in the macro.

❷ The remaining shows the output from the `macro` command, including a list of all the commands that are included in the macro.

The macro is now created. To execute it, simply type the macro's name:

```
>>> quickinit    ❶
>>> img.show()   ❷
```

❶ The `quickinit` macro was created in the previous code block.

❷ The `img` object was created by the `quickinit` macro.

To see a list of previously created macros, type the `macro` command with no parameters:

```
>>> macro
['quickinit']
```

Because only one macro was previously created, only one is displayed. If more are created, they would also be listed there. If you want to save a macro to use in other sessions, you can use the `store` command. In addition, to see a list of all the commands that were included in a previously created macro, use the `print` command followed by the name of the macro. To show the commands from the previously created `quickinit` macro:

```
>>> print quickinit   ❶
from SimpleCV import Camera   ❷
cam = Camera()
img = cam.getImage()
```

❶ The `print` command followed by a macro name lists all of the commands in a macro.

❷ This is an output of the print macro command.

The above example is probably a bit inefficient. It is not necessary to import the Camera library every time. In fact, the SimpleCV shell automatically loads all of SimpleCV's libraries, so no import statement is even needed. Fortunately, it is possible to edit a previously created macro using the `edit` command.

```
>>> edit quickinit
```

On many Mac and Linux systems, the default editor for the `edit` command is VI. VI is not the world's easiest editor for casual users. For more information on using VI, visit *http://www.vim.org* and click on the link for their documentation. It can be easy to get stuck on even basic commands like saving or quitting. As a quick hint to those who may be stuck, press i when in VI in order to enter insert mode to edit the file. To exit insert mode, press escape to be switched back to command mode. From command mode, save the changes and quit VI by entering :wq (as in write-quit).

Run and Edit Python Scripts

The SimpleCV shell can also be used to work with external Python scripts. This can be helpful when testing and debugging files. For example, assume that the photo booth demo from Chapter 2 is saved in a file named *photobooth.py*. To run this from inside the shell, simply type:

```
>>> run photobooth.py
```

This will startup and run the photo booth application. To stop the execution, either click the close button on the window, or hit Control-C from inside the shell.

Notice that the messages in the application appear in a very small font in the middle of the screen. Wouldn't it be better to increase the font size and put the message in the corner? It is easy to open and edit files directly in the shell. In fact, this was already demonstrated earlier. Simply type:

```
>>> edit photobooth.py
```

This opens the editor. Now go down to line 13 and change the previous `drawText()` command to:

```
img.drawText("Starting app.  Left click to save photo", 0, 0, fontsize=50,
color=Color().getRandom())
```

Next, go to line 30 to find the other `drawText()` command and change it to:

```
img.drawText("Took a photo.  Click the mouse to take another.", 0, 0, fontsize=50,
color=Color().getRandom())
```

Now save and exit. The shell will save the file and instantly relaunch the program. This is rather convenient when repeatedly jumping back and forth between editing a file and then running to test the file.

Timing

Some of the feature detection and template matching algorithms can be complex and computationally intensive algorithms. When time matters, it is important to understand how long it takes a program to execute. For example, consider a security camera designed to detect people walking into a room. If the program takes five seconds just to process one image, then a person could sneak by between frames. Or another case where speed would matter would be a camera on an assembly line that needs to capture and process images fast enough to keep up with the flow of products. Fortunately, it is fairly easy to test a program, identify the bottlenecks, and tune the program to better align with the software design requirements.

The `timeit` function is used to time a given function. To see a basic example of how this works, consider a basic blob detection example. This appears to run pretty quickly, but how fast? Use the `timeit()` function to find out:

```
>>> img = Image('logo')
>>> %timeit blobs = img.findBlobs(100)  ❶
```

❶ Notice that `timeit` was added to the beginning of this line. As a result, this line of code will be timed.

The `timeit` function actually runs the specified line of code 100 times and find the best times. The output from the function will be something like: **100 loops, best of 3: 2.12 ms per loop**. This means that it takes 2.12 milliseconds to run that snippet of code. (Actual output will vary from computer to computer.) Not too bad.

But still, the logo image is kind of small. It it relatively easy to find blobs on a small image because there is less data to process. What about for a larger image? For example, an HD camera could be capturing images that are 1920×1280. How much longer will that take? The SimpleCV shell does not ship with a 1920×1280 version of an image, but it is possible to fake one by scaling the built-in image to those dimensions.

```
>>> img = Image('logo')
>>> imgHD = img.resize(1920, 1280)  ❶
>>> %timeit blobs = imgHD.findBlobs(100)
```

❶ This scales the image to 1920×1280.

In this case, the computing time was 41.7 ms. Once again, the actual output time will vary, but it will probably require about 20 times more processing time than the original image. 40 milliseconds is still pretty quick, but this is a single line of code on a pretty simple image.

 Need to speed up a program? One trick is to shrink the image size. For example, a 640×480 image is a lot easier to process than a full HD image.

Cameras and Lenses

Chapter 5 discussed the importance of lighting in a vision system. Of course, even the best lighting system will run into problems if the system is using the wrong camera. This appendix provides a brief introduction to some of the issues when choosing a camera. It covers:

- Basics of digital cameras
- A background on lenses

Cameras and Digital Sensors

Cameras have sensors that measure incoming light levels and then map that light onto a grid to form an image. Before digital photography became dominant, this process was done chemically, where the chemicals on the film would react to the light coming through the lens. Today, digital cameras have replaced chemicals with millions of little sensors that detect incoming light.

There are two commonly used digital light sensors: Charge Coupled Device (CCD) and Complementary Metal Oxide Semiconductor (CMOS):

- CCD is the most commonly used sensor in digital cameras. As a general rule, they create good quality, low noise images. However, they tend to require more power, making them less popular for cell phones, tablet computers, and other portable devices.
- CMOS uses less power than CCD. This means they are rapidly gaining in popularity as cameras are included in many battery powered devices. However, CMOS tends to result in lower quality and higher noise images. In addition, they are less light sensitive, which means they do not work well in low-light conditions.

Light sensors are color blind. To create color, light must be broken into the primary colors: red, green and blue. One approach is to use color filters, which rapidly rotate through the three colors in the hopes of capturing identical images filtered by color. This approach will be problematic if the object being photographed is rapidly moving.

An alternative is a beam splitter. This splits the light beam into its red, green, and blue components, which are then sent to sensors for each color. Although this solves problems inherent in color filters, it adds bulk to the camera, which is problematic with small devices. To resolve these problems, many cameras instead have adjacent pixels capture different colors. One pixel captures red information, an adjacent pixel captures green information, and a third pixel captures the blue information. This approach is called a *Bayer Filter*, as demonstrated in Figure B-1. As long as the pixels are small enough, the independent pixel colors can be blended together to form the appropriate combined colors.

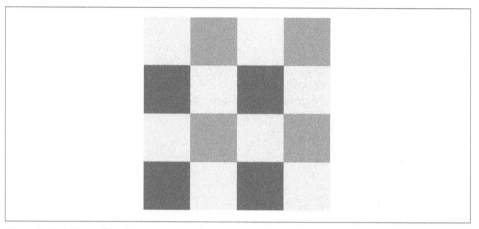

Figure B-1. A Bayer filter for capturing color

Like film-based cameras, digital light sensors are affected by the amount of time they are exposed to light. In a film camera, exposure time referred to the amount of time the shutter was opened, therefore exposing the chemicals to the light. Digital cameras do not need a physical shutter. Instead, exposure time in a digital camera refers to the time frame in which the sensors are exposed to the light, collecting information about light levels, before the values are digitally reset and the process begins again.

As a final note for this section, most modern consumer-level cameras are marketed based on megapixels. One megapixel equals a million pixels. It measures the number of points the image sensor can capture. This is usually a poor proxy for the overall quality of the camera. Putting a cheap lens in front of a high megapixel sensor merely results in a detailed capture of a rotten image. Most people cannot tell the difference between a cheap low megapixel image and an expensive high megapixel image. More megapixels can be helpful when cropping, zooming, and other types of slicing and dicing, but megapixels are a weak indicator of the quality of the camera.

Lenses

The final piece of the puzzle is the lens. Lenses are curved pieces of glass designed to direct light onto the camera's sensor. Not all lenses are created equal. In addition to the common issues of zoom and focus, camera lenses can have unintended effects on your images. In the process of bending the light, a camera lens can also alter the contrast and color of the image, or create other anomalies. To help correct for these aberrations, most lenses are actually combinations of lenses. Most of these corrections are beyond the control of the camera operator, except to the extent that good camera lenses cost more money. Cheap lenses mean lower quality pictures.

The primary job of the camera lens is to focus the image on the camera's image sensor, as demonstrated in Figure B-2. All of the incoming light should converge on the camera sensor. If the light converges ahead of or behind the sensor, then the image will be out of focus. If the image is not in focus, the lens is moved slightly forward or backwards until the image converges on the sensor.

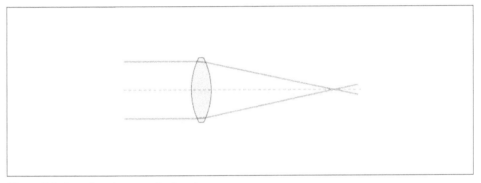

Figure B-2. Lens focusing on a single point

In addition to focusing the image, lenses are also responsible for controlling how much of the field of view the camera sees. This is based on the focal length of the camera. The focal length refers to the distance between the lens and the focal point where the image converges. If the image converges on the sensor, then the image will be in focus. Short focal lengths correspond to wide angles of view. Long focal lengths correspond to greater magnification and a smaller field of view. Figure B-3 shows the changing field of view and zoom-level for a camera taking pictures of a compass. Note, however, that most zoom lenses can perform more complex operations than simply varying the distance between the lens and the sensor.

Many consumer-grade webcams are designed to focus on objects a couple of feet away —approximately the distance between a computer monitor and a person sitting at the computer—and therefore have limited or no ability to adjust their zoom level. However, they may be able to fake a zoom using digital techniques. Digital zoom has nothing to do with the camera's lens. Instead, a digital zoom essentially crops the picture to the

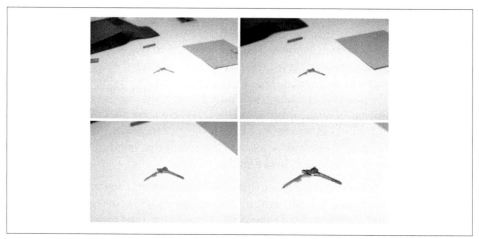

Figure B-3. Image of a compass, taken with different focal lengths

"zoomed" region and then resizes it to fill the same dimensions as the original image. Because such tricks can result in a pixelated image, most systems apply various smoothing algorithms to the image at the same time.

In addition to the focal length, lenses are also measured based on their *aperture*. This measures the size of the opening allowing in light. Aperture is usually measured as *f-numbers*, which are the ratio of the focal length to the aperture diameter. The smaller the f-number, the greater the aperture.

The obvious effect of aperture is to control the amount of light that reaches the camera's sensor. The actual amount of light that hits the sensor is also controlled by the exposure time. A fast exposure requires a larger aperture to ensure that enough light reaches the sensor. In contrast, the aperture may need to be reduced with a slow exposure time to ensure that the image is not blown out with too much light.

In addition to affecting the amount of light reaching the sensor, aperture also affects the depth of field. This refers to how far away an object can be from the camera while still being in focus. In slightly technical terms, this is the result of *collimated light*. Collimated light refers to light traveling in nice, neat, parallel paths. Most light is bouncing around the environment, following many different paths. But it is easiest to clearly focus collimated light, especially when looking at distant objects. Closing the aperture results in more collimated light, as only light traveling in the right direction can make it through the smaller opening. This in turn makes it easier to focus on more distant objects.

Once again, webcams provide limited control over aperture. Instead of controlling the amount of light entering the camera via the aperture, most webcams use digital post processing to adjust the brightness. This often involves brightening tricks, such as described in Chapter 6, where images can be brightened by adding or multiplying values to their pixels.

Advanced Features

This appendix covers a few of the more advanced segmentation and feature extraction tools in the SimpleCV framework. Some of these automate basic processes covered earlier in the book, such as looking at the differences between sets of images. Other elements represent more advanced tools for identifying and extracting features.

Foreground/Background Segmentation

As we mentioned in Chapter 8, the purpose of feature detection is to identify the parts of an image that are "interesting." It might seem counterintuitive, but one way to determine what is interesting is to first find what is uninteresting. Remove what is uninteresting in an image and the interesting portion must be part of what is left. This is a useful technique because sometimes it's easier to identify the uninteresting parts of an image—namely the background. For instance, given video feed, the moving parts of the image are often the interesting parts and the stationary parts are less interesting.

In computer vision, this type of process is called foreground/background segmentation, and there are a variety of ways to accomplish it. The SimpleCV framework currently supports three different techniques:

- frame differencing segmentation
- running segmentation, and
- color segmentation

All of these methods examine multiple images to find pixels that are changing (the foreground) versus the pixels that remain static (the background). Also remember that the terms foreground and background do not refer to how far away from the camera an object is. Instead, foreground represents the interesting part of the image that should be processed and the background is everything else.

Frame Differencing Segmentation

The first method is frame differencing segmentation. Difference segmentation takes two or more images and finds the differences between them. It then applies a threshold to the differences, and keeps all of the pixels that meet the threshold requirements as being significantly different. This method is exceptionally fast, but it does have its limitations. For instance, while it's designed to find moving objects, it will have a difficult time locating objects that are moving slowly as there will not be much changing from one image to the next. It's also susceptible to noise in the images and to a lot of variance in lighting conditions.

In contrast to some of the feature extractors and segmentation tools from the previous chapters, difference segmentation follows a slightly different pattern. The general steps are as follows:

- Create a `DiffSegmentation` object that handles the image comparisons
- Add images to the `DiffSegmentation` object created in the previous step
- After the segmenter has enough images to compare (at least two images), use the `getSegmentedImage()` function to extract an image that represents the difference between the previous images

 If the segmenter does not have enough images to find a significant difference, the `getSegmentedImage()` function returns `None`.

The example below demonstrates frame differencing segmentation. This example code looks for the largest moving object captured by the camera.

```
from SimpleCV import Camera, Color, DiffSegmentation, Display

cam = Camera()
firstImg = cam.getImage()

ds = DiffSegmentation()      ❶
ds.addImage(firstImg)        ❷

disp = Display(firstImg.size())

while disp.isNotDone():
    img = cam.getImage()
    ds.addImage(img)         ❸

    diffImg = ds.getSegmentedImage(False)   ❹

    if diffImg is not None:   ❺
```

```
blobs = diffImg.dilate(3).findBlobs()   ❻
if( blobs is not None ):
    img.dl().polygon(blobs[-1].mConvexHull,color=Color.RED)   ❼

img.save(disp)
```

❶ The first step is to create a `DiffSegmentation` object. This will handle the segmentation process on the images.

❷ Add the first image to the `DiffSegmentation` object with the `addImage()` function. This first image is also used in the next line to calibrate the `Display` size.

❸ While the display is active, the `while` loop will have the camera continue to capture images and then add them to the segmenter.

❹ Get the segmented image. By default, this returns an image where white represents the foreground and black represents the background. By passing `getSegmented Image` the false argument, the image is inverted so that black represents the foreground, and white the background.

❺ If the segmenter did not have enough images to return a result, it returns `None`. This `if` statement checks to see if there is enough information to proceed.

❻ Clean up the segmented binary image by dilating it and then find any blobs in the image.

❼ Finally, indicate the region of interest by drawing a red box around it.

The result should look like Figure C-1. Notice that the region bounded by the red lines represents the region where motion was detected.

Figure C-1. Motion found with difference segmentation

Running Segmentation

Running segmentation is similar to frame differencing, but instead of comparing two frames, it compares the current frame to a model frame. The model frame is a weighted average from the sequence of the previous frames. As a result, this approach is slightly slower than frame differencing, but produces slightly more robust results. The RunningSegmentation algorithm takes two arguments:

alpha
> This controls how the previous sequence of images is combined to form the model frame. By default, the value is 0.7, or 70%. This means the model frame is updated by taking 30% of the newest image plus 70% of the previous model frame.

threshold
> Determines if an object in the foreground or the background. This works the same as the threshold parameter of the binarize() function for Image objects. It can either be a single integer or a tuple to separately threshold the (R, G, B) parameters.

```
from SimpleCV import Camera, Color, RunningSegmentation, Display

cam = Camera()

firstImg = cam.getImage()

rs = RunningSegmentation(alpha=0.5)   ❶

rs.addImage(firstImg)   ❷

disp = Display(firstImg.size())

while disp.isNotDone():
    img = cam.getImage()

    rs.addImage(img)

    diffImg = rs.getSegmentedImage(False)

    if diffImg is not None:   ❸

        blobs = diffImg.dilate(3).findBlobs()

        if( blobs is not None ):
            img.dl().polygon(blobs[-1].mConvexHull,color=Color.RED)

    img.save(disp)
```

❶ Creates the RunningSegmentation object with an alpha of 0.5. This means that the model frame will consist of 50% of the most recently added frame and 50% of the previous frames.

❷ Add the first image to the RunningSegmentation object.

❸ Double-check to make sure that the segmenter received enough images to return a result.

Color Segmentation

We worked with color segmentation in previous chapters, but those methods were focused on segmenting a single color. Although it is possible to apply those methods repeatedly to detect multiple colors, it would be a cumbersome process. Instead, the SimpleCV framework has a `ColorSegmentation` library that makes it easier to perform these types of tasks.

The overall pattern of use for Color Segmentation is similar to the Difference Segmentation and Running Segmentation approaches, but it has a twist: the model must first be trained to know which colors to look for. The model is trained by providing images with the colors that represent foreground images. Once the model is trained, colors that were not in the training set will be considered background colors. The role of the segmentation algorithm is to then find the sections of the image that match the trained colors. The revised program flow for color segmentation is:

1. Create a `ColorSegmentation` object.
2. Train it by adding images with the `addToModel()` function.
3. Add the image to be segmented by using the `addImage()` function.
4. Get the resulting segmented image by using the `getSegmentedImage()` function.

The following block of example code is an outline for a basic card game involving a set of flash cards. The player must decide if the flash card's text color is a primary color (red, green, or blue). As a twist, the text on the card names a color, but this color is not always the same as the font's actual color. For example, the card could have the word *Red* printed on it, with the text written in green. For this introductory example, the computer simply finds the answer and shows it on the screen. A longer example is provided at the end of this appendix to create a more interactive version.

```
from SimpleCV import ColorSegmentation, Image, ImageSet
import time

redBlock = Image('redBlock.png')   ❶
greenBlock = Image('greenBlock.png')
blueBlock = Image('blueBlock.png')

cs = ColorSegmentation()   ❷

cs.addToModel(redBlock)   ❸
cs.addToModel(greenBlock)
cs.addToModel(blueBlock)

cards = ImageSet('cards')   ❹
```

```
for card in cards:
    cs.addImage(card)   ❺

    res = cs.getSegmentedImage()   ❻

    color = res.meanColor()   ❼

    if ((color[0] < 254) and (color[1] < 254) and (color[2] < 254)):
        card.drawText('Primary Color!', 0, 0)
    else:
        card.drawText('Not primary', 0, 0)

    card.show()
    time.sleep(5)
```

❶ The *redBlock.png*, *greenBlock.png*, and *blueBlock.png* images are the three training images. They will train the segmentation algorithm that pure red, green, and blue are foreground colors. All other colors will then be considered background colors.

❷ Creates the ColorSegmentation object.

❸ Adds the training images for the color segmentation.

❹ Load an image set with the example flash cards. Two of the cards are written in a primary color. One is not.

❺ Add the card image to be checked.

❻ Gets the results of the color segmentation. By default, the getSegmentedImage() function returns a binary image when the background is white and the foreground is black. If False had been passed in as an argument to getSegmentedImage(), the resulting image would be reversed so that black would be the background and white would be the foreground.

❼ This line checks the mean color of the segmented image. If none of the training colors were found, then the image is considered all background, resulting in a purely white image. If a training color was found, then it appears in black, which will result in a lower mean color. Note that while technically a white background would be (255, 255, 255), we test against (254, 254, 254) to allow for a small amount of noise in the processing.

An example of the output is shown in Figure C-2. The text is written in red, so it places the message, "Primary Color!" in the upper-left corner of the image.

Feature Extractors

Some image features are slightly less straightforward than the shape- or template-based features discussed up to this point. These features can be the hues that make up an image, or the direction and length of edges in a region of an image. In the SimpleCV

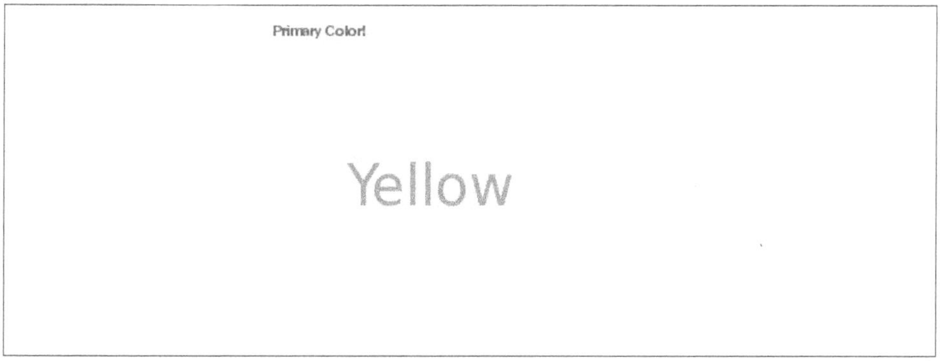

Primary Color!

Yellow

Figure C-2. An example of the color segmentation output

framework, these features are abstracted into feature vectors, which are simply lists of numbers that define some attribute of an image.

Feature vectors are obtained by using a feature extractor, which returns a NumPy array of the values. The SimpleCV machine learning library uses these feature vectors to classify objects. Each feature extractor has three methods associated with it:

extract()
> Takes in an image and returns a feature vector

getFieldNames()
> Returns the name of each value of the feature vector

getNumFields()
> Returns the total number of features in the feature vector

In order to better understand these features extractors, lets assume that there is a hypothetical extractor named FruitFeatureExtractor. This FruitFeatureExtractor is designed to work with red apples and yellow bananas, and returns a list of two numbers: a color and shape value. The color is a scale from -1 (yellow) to 1 (red). The shape measure how oblong the fruit is, with -1 for long and skinny like a pencil, and +1 if the fruit is perfectly round. Figure C-3 gives a good example of what this fruit feature space looks like plotted on an x, y axis.

Based on the graph, almost all apples have positive values for both color and shape, while all bananas have negative values. This system could them be used to sort fruit at a hypothetical fruit plantation. To classify fruit, the FruitFeatureExtractor examines the shape and color, and then checks if the returned values are closer to (1, 1), representing an apple, or to (-1, -1), representing a banana (see Figure C-4).

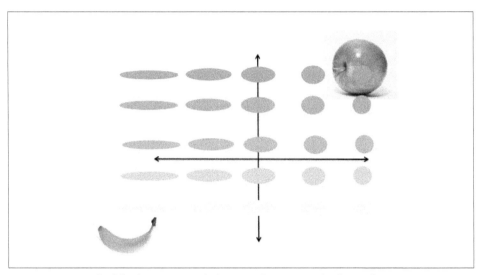

Figure C-3. A graph of the fruit space, with shape on the x-axis and color on the y-axis

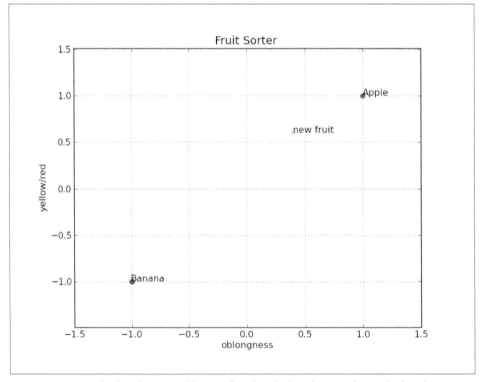

Figure C-4. Example plot of a piece of fruit to classify, which is closer to the Apple classification

The fruit feature extractor is a little silly and packed with assumptions, so it's not likely to ever be implemented in a real-world context. However, the SimpleCV library includes other, more useful feature extractors. The following sections describe them in more detail.

Edge Histograms

The edge histogram feature vector extractor takes an input image and applies an edge detector, as described in the previous chapter. Then it finds the length of each edge, as well as the edge angles. If the length of the edges was saved as is, then images of different size would have different lengths for the same feature. In order to make the edge vectors more comparable between images, the lengths of each edge are normalized using half of the largest dimension of the input image. These normalized edge lengths are combined with the edge angles to create the final edge histogram feature set.

The example code below uses pictures of cars, such as those shown in Figure C-5, and compares the edge histograms to identify the model. It starts by extracting the edge histogram for the car we want to identify, and then calculates the edge histograms for the two reference images. The code then compares each histogram by computing the sum of the square of the differences between each histogram. We first square the different edge values to remove the impact from any negative numbers, and then sum them together because it's the combination of all of the edges that describes the car as a whole.

Figure C-5. Which two pictures are the most similar?

By default, the edge histogram detector is configured as two sets of bins, a bin of 10 edge lengths and a bin of 10 angles, each appended into a single list of 20 elements. This can also be configured by passing a parameter to the constructor, such as Edge HistogramFeatureExtractor(15), which will instead use a bin of 15 lengths and a bin of 15 angles.

```
from SimpleCV import Image, np

# The car to test
compare = Image("explorer1.png")

# The two images to compare it to
img1 = Image('explorer2.png')
```

```
img2 = Image('focus.png')

edgeFeats = EdgeHistogramFeatureExtractor()  ❶

a = np.array(edgeFeats.extract(compare))  ❷
b = np.array(edgeFeats.extract(img1))
c = np.array(edgeFeats.extract(img2))

AandB = np.sum(np.square((a-b)))  ❸

AandC = np.sum(np.square((a-c)))

AandB  ❹
# Will output 0.10205....

AandC
# Will output 1.21376
```

❶ First, extract the edge histogram for the image of the car using the `EdgeHistogram FeatureExtractor()` function.

❷ The `extract()` function extracts the values of the features in the image, and returns the values as a NumPy array. The NumPy array allows for fast computations when comparing the feature vectors.

❸ Now compute the sum of the squared distances. In other words, determine how similar the features in the images are.

❹ Output the calculation results. Smaller values mean that the images are more alike because there is a smaller difference between the features. The results show that the two Ford Explorers are more alike than when the Ford Explorer is compared to the Ford Focus.

Haar Features

Haar features were introduced in Chapter 10 in the context of face detection. For tasks like face detection, a large number of Haar features are combined to form a Haar Cascade. That cascade then serves as a template for detecting faces in other images. Even without a full Haar Cascade, however, the underlying Haar features can be extracted from an image. A Haar feature is a way of categorizing subsections of an image. Think of it as a process that takes a square or rectangle and divides it into two parts. The square is placed over various points on the image. First the pixels in each part of the square are summed. Then the sum of the pixels from the first part is subtracted from the sub of the pixels in the second part. For example, consider the top left image of Figure C-6. Objects that are symmetrical about the x-axis have very low values, while objects that are asymmetric about this axis have very large values.

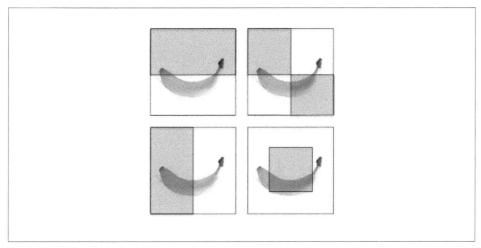

Figure C-6. Haar-like Wavelets applied to a banana

The creation of Haar features requires a configuration file. This file defines how the aforementioned squares are arranged on image to detect the features. The SimpleCV framework ships with a default wavelets file named *haar.txt* located in the SimpleCV features directory. The Haar feature extractor works in a similar fashion to the previous feature extractor examples, as demonstrated in the next example.

This example uses Haar features to detect the difference between bows. Or, to be more accurate, it tells the difference between the pretty ribbon bows that are placed on presents versus the type of bow that is used to shoot arrows. The example images are shown in Figure C-7. The example code will compare the three images and should presumably find that the two ribbon bows are alike.

Figure C-7. Left: A red bow; Center: A blue bow; Right: A longbow

```
from SimpleCV import Image, HaarLikeFeatureExtractor, np

redbow = Image('redbow.png')  ❶
bluebow = Image('bluebow.png')
longbow = Image('longbow.png')

haar = HaarLikeFeatureExtractor('haar.txt')  ❷

a = np.array(haar.extract(redbow))  ❸
b = np.array(haar.extract(bluebow))
c = np.array(haar.extract(longbow))

AandB = np.sum(np.square(a-b))  ❹
AandC = np.sum(np.square(a-c))
BandC = np.sum(np.square(b-c))

print AandB  ❺
# Outputs 6.47x10^13
print AandC
# Outputs 4.52x10^14
print BandC
# Outputs 5.16x10^14
```

❶ First, load the images to be compared.

❷ Initialize the Haar feature detector with the built-in Haar wavelet file.

❸ Just like the previous feature extractor example, pass the images to the Haar feature extract to get the feature.

❹ Compute the difference between each feature. Smaller numbers mean the features are more similar.

❺ Not surprisingly, the two pictures of ribbon bows are the most alike. Their distance is an order of magnitude less than the other combinations.

Hue Histogram

The hue histogram feature extractor, HueHistogramFeatureExtractor(), works in a similar fashion to the edge histogram method. It builds a histogram of hue values for comparing images based on their hue. This feature extractor divides all of the hues of the rainbow into 16 bins. It then classifies each pixel's hue based on these 16 bins. Revisiting the previous example, here's how to do it using the image hues instead:

```
from SimpleCV import Image, HueHistogramFeatureExtractor, np

redbow = Image('redbow.png')  ❶
bluebow = Image('bluebow.png')
longbow = Image('longbow.png')

hue = HueHistogramFeatureExtractor()  ❷
```

```
a = np.array(hue.extract(redbow))  ❸
b = np.array(hue.extract(bluebow))
c = np.array(hue.extract(longbow))

AandB = np.sum(np.square(a-b))  ❹
AandC = np.sum(np.square(a-c))
BandC = np.sum(np.square(b-c))

print AandB
# Outputs 0.0036
print AandC
# Outputs 0.0030
print BandC
# Outputs 0.0001
```

❶ Load the images. Once again, the first two are ribbons for presents. The third is an image of a longbow. Note, however, that one of the bows is blue and the longbow image also has a lot of blue.

❷ Create a `HueHistogramFeatureExtractor` object. If desired, the number of bins for the histogram can be passed as an argument to this constructor.

❸ Extract the features.

❹ Compare the images by computing the distance between their features, just like with the other types of feature extractors.

When using the Haar feature extractor, the two ribbons were the most similar. When using the Hue Histogram feature extractor, the blue ribbon matches more closely with the blue background on the longbow image.

Morphology Revisited

Morphology is covered in the book in the context of cleaning up noise in an image. Another role for morphology is comparing two objects based on their shape. In the SimpleCV framework, morphology information is extracted in several steps. In addition to the basic `MorphologyFeatureExtractor()` function, which works like the other feature extractor constructors, it also requires a threshold function, which helps to identify the shape to be measured. In many cases, this function can be a simple `binarize()` operation, perhaps with other basic image manipulation. This function is then passed as a parameter to the `setThresholdOperation()` operation function of the `MorphologyFeatureExtractor`.

It may be easier to understand this by looking at a little code, as shown in the next example. This example looks at the shapes of a set of toy blocks. The blocks to be compared are shown in Figure C-8.

Figure C-8. Toy blocks for shape comparison

```
from SimpleCV import Image, MorphologyFeatureExtractor, np

def myBinaryFunc(input):    ❶
    return input.binarize().erode()

block = Image('bluesquare.png')    ❷
heart = Image('redheart.png')
circle = Image('greencirc.png')

mf = MorphologyFeatureExtractor()    ❸
mf.setThresholdOperation(myBinaryFunc)    ❹

a = np.array(mf.extract(block))    ❺
b = np.array(mf.extract(heart))
c = np.array(mf.extract(circle))

AandB = np.sum(np.square(a-b))    ❻
AandC = np.sum(np.square(a-c))
BandC = np.sum(np.square(b-c))

print AandB
# Outputs 5.672
print AandC
# Outputs 9.196
print BandC
# Outputs 0.427
```

❶ This is the threshold function required by the feature extractor. It does a fairly straightforward binarization, with an erosion to clean up noise in the image.

❷ Load the set of images with objects that need to be compared.

❸ Initialize the `MorphologyFeatureExtractor()`, similar to the other feature extractors.

❹ This is a different step when compared with other feature extractors. This is where the threshold function is set. Pass the function as a parameter to `setThresholdOper ation()`.

❺ Extract the features.

❻ Once again, compare the images by computing the distance between their features.

Examples

Most of the examples provided in this appendix have relied on static images with no user feedback. The following two examples provide a more dynamic user interaction. They include:

- A target tracking example, which keeps a set of crosshairs pointed at any object that moves in the webcam's view.
- A flashcard game based on the color of the text on the card.

Target Tracking

The following example is a basic target tracking system. It looks for an object that moves, finds the center of that object, and moves the crosshairs to that point.

```
from SimpleCV import Camera, Color, Display, RunningSegmentation

cam = Camera()
rs = RunningSegmentation(.5)

size = (cam.getImage().size())
disp = Display(size)

# Start the crosshairs in the center of the screen
center = (size[0] / 2, size[1] / 2)

while disp.isNotDone():
    input = cam.getImage()
    # Assume using monitor mounted camera, so flip to create mirror image
    input = input.flipHorizontal()
    rs.addImage(input)  # ❶

    if(rs.isReady()):
        # Get the object that moved
        img = rs.getSegmentedImage(False)  # ❷
        blobs = img.dilate(3).findBlobs()

        # If a object in motion was found
        if( blobs is not None ):
            blobs = blobs.sortArea()
            # Update the crosshairs onto the object in motion
            center = (int(blobs[-1].minRectX()),
                        int(blobs[-1].minRectY()))  # ❸

        # Inside circle
        input.dl().circle(center, 50, Color.BLACK, width = 3)  # ❹
        # Outside circle
        input.dl().circle(center, 200, Color.BLACK, width = 6)

        # Radiating lines
        input.dl().line((center[0], center[1] - 50),
                        (center[0], 0), Color.BLACK, width = 2)
```

```
input.dl().line((center[0], center[1] + 50),
                (center[0], size[1]), Color.BLACK, width = 2)
input.dl().line((center[0] - 50, center[1]),
                (0, center[1]), Color.BLACK, width = 2)
input.dl().line((center[0] + 50, center[1]),
                (size[0], center[1]), Color.BLACK, width = 2)

input.save(disp)
```

❶ Add the image to the segmentation object to detect if anything is new.

❷ Get the output image that shows the object that changed from the previous image.

❸ Set the new crosshairs center to be the middle of the bounding box of the changed object. Note that the center point must be typecast to integers because the coordinates for the drawing must be expressed in integers.

❹ Finally, draw the crosshairs, similar to what was done in Chapter 7.

An example of the output is shown in Figure C-9.

Figure C-9. Example output from targeting system

Color Game

The following example builds on the color game from the ColorSegmentation section. Whereas the earlier section only did the basics to test the card, now the user can interact with the system. Click the left mouse button if the text on the card is written in red, green, or blue. Otherwise, click the right button.

```
from SimpleCV import ColorSegmentation, Display, Image, ImageSet
import time

redBlock = Image('redblock.png')
greenBlock = Image('greenBlock.png')
blueBlock = Image('blueBlock.png')

cs = ColorSegmentation()
cs.addToModel(redBlock)
cs.addToModel(greenBlock)
cs.addToModel(blueBlock)

cards = ImageSet('cards')
card = None

disp = Display((320, 240))

score = 0
isPrimary = False

while (cards or card) and disp.isNotDone():

    if card is None:
        card = cards.pop()

        cs.addImage(card)
        res = cs.getSegmentedImage()

        color = res.meanColor()
        if ((color[0] < 254) and (color[1] < 254) and (color[2] < 254)):
            isPrimary = True
        else:
            isPrimary = False

        card.drawText('Click left if primary, otherwise right', 0, 0)
        card.drawText(str(score) + ' correct answers', 0, 210)

    card.save(disp)

    if disp.mouseLeft:
        if isPrimary:
            card.drawText('Correct!', fontsize=30)
            score += 1
        else:
            card.drawText('Wrong!', fontsize=30)

        card.save(disp)
        time.sleep(2)
        card = None

    if disp.mouseRight:
        if not isPrimary:
```

```
        card.drawText('Correct!', fontsize=30)
        score += 1
    else:
        card.drawText('Wrong!', fontsize=30)

    card.save(disp)
    time.sleep(2)
    card = None
```

A demonstration of the output is shown in Figure C-10.

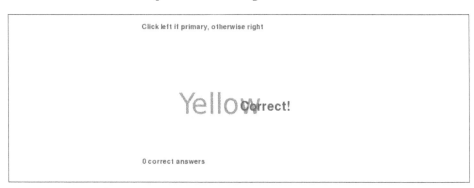

Figure C-10. Example game output

About the Authors

Kurt DeMaagd is a technology entrepreneur. Kurt was a co-founder of Slashdot, and a professor at Michigan State University where he taught and conducted research in information management, economics, and policy. He has published works related to decision support systems, net neutrality, and IT for economic development.

Anthony Oliver is an advocate for modern web technology in industry, and a vision system aficionado. He has worked in machine vision and robotics for five years with the Big Three automakers as well as other large manufacturers. He has been involved with technical and open source communities his entire professional career, and has written several articles on machine vision.

Nathan Oostendorp is the founder of Sight Machine. He has over fifteen years worth of experience running open source communities, serving as one of the founders of Slashdot, the site director for SourceForge, and the creator of the online communities PerlMonks and Everything2. His areas of expertise include software architecture, information economics, incentive design, and large-scale information system operation.

Katherine Scott has over ten years experience working as a research engineer for a number of military research projects covering the domains of computer vision, robotics, augmented reality, and simulation. She holds bachelor of science and engineering degrees in both computer engineering and electrical engineering from the University of Michigan, Ann Arbor, as well as a master's degree in computer science with a concentration in computer vision and graphics from Columbia University.

Have it your way.